FEARLESS

FEARLESS

How an Underdog Becomes a Champion

DOUG PEDERSON

WITH DAN POMPEI

hachette
BOOKS

NEW YORK   BOSTON

Hachette Books
Hachette Book Group
1290 Avenue of the Americas, New York, NY 10104
hachettebooks.com
twitter.com/hachettebooks

Originally published in hardcover and ebook by Hachette Books in August 2018.
First trade paperback edition: August 2019

Hachette Books is an imprint of Perseus Books, LLC, a subsidiary of Hachette Book Group, Inc. The Hachette Books name and logo are trademarks of Hachette Book Group, Inc.

The publisher is not responsible for websites (or their content) that are not owned by the publisher.

The Hachette Speakers Bureau provides a wide range of authors for speaking events. To find out more, go to www.hachettespeakersbureau.com or call (866) 376-6591.

LCCN: 2018945258
ISBN: 978-0-316-45165-9

Printed in the United States of America

LSC-C

10 9 8 7 6 5 4 3 2 1

CONTENTS

FOREWORD

When Doug Pederson interviewed for our head coaching position, he was the offensive coordinator for the Kansas City Chiefs, who had just beaten the Houston Texans in the Wild Card Round of the playoffs. In just six days, they would be playing the Patriots, so I understood that he would not be able to focus his full attention on the interview process and express the type of head coach he envisioned himself to be. But there were still many things that stood out to us and that came across very clearly during our time with him. He had a lot of confidence but in a way that was the opposite of arrogance. He communicated very well. He was very honest.

He was very comfortable with himself. He wasn't trying to impress anyone. He was just being himself.

That meant something. For a football coach, being able to listen, relate, and communicate is crucial. So is the ability to gain the confidence of those around you and establish trust on both a strategic level and an emotional level. In today's world, many of the most successful head coaches can relate to the players they are working with and developing. I could see Doug had that ability, and that was important to me.

I had known Doug since he was our quarterback sixteen years earlier. We had signed him as a free agent to be our starter in 1999, and then we drafted Donovan McNabb. I remember how comfortable he was in what could be a difficult situation. He was very committed to helping develop Donovan and he still was able to prepare and perform like the gritty quarterback he was. There was an unselfishness about him that gave us an inkling of what kind of coach he could be.

Ten years after Doug played for the Eagles, he returned as an assistant coach under Andy Reid. That's when I noticed how diligent he was, how focused he was, and how much attention he paid to details. It was clear he had a real feel for the offensive game. I always enjoyed his evaluations of quarterbacks leading up to the draft. It was interesting to hear his perspective on those guys every year. In addition, he was always looking to teach on the field. On a few occasions, after practice, Doug even approached my then thirteen-year-old son to work with him on his quarterback mechanics. You could see how much he enjoyed coaching and how easy it came to him.

So when we set out to hire a head coach in 2016, I thought back to my previous experiences with Doug. I had believed for a while that he had the ingredients I was looking for in a head coach. I had seen the vision developing for years. But what I didn't know was how much he had evolved as a coach during his time as an offensive coordinator in Kansas City.

In order to find out how he developed during his three years there, I spent hours talking to Andy Reid. Howie Roseman, our general manager, did the same thing separately. I was able to spend a few hours interviewing Coach Pederson, but Andy had been interviewing Doug for years—every day at work, both in Philadelphia and Kansas City. Speaking with Andy was a real opportunity to gain more knowledge about a candidate than you ever could in a normal interview process. We discussed all of the attributes a head coach requires to be successful. I questioned everything. How does he handle quarterbacks? How is he in front of the whole room? What is his approach to the offense? Is he creative? Is he risk averse? Is he sensitive to criticism? How does he communicate with other coaches? How does he communicate with players from different backgrounds? We talked about multiple players on the Chiefs and how he related to them. We also went back to some players on the Eagles that we both knew. The conversations were very detailed, and gave me a great understanding of where Doug was as a coach.

I also asked Andy how Doug would handle a losing streak, because even successful teams go through difficult stretches from time to time. Andy talked about a five-game losing streak the Chiefs had during the 2015 season and he said Doug was the most even-keeled coach on the staff. You couldn't tell whether the team was on a winning streak or a losing streak from being around him. I thought back to that during the 2017 season when we lost so many key players to injuries, including our great young quarterback Carson Wentz. At no moment was Doug ever flustered. He always just went back to the drawing board to try to figure out how to deal with the loss and maximize the players who were available. Just as Andy Reid had told me, Doug was unflappable.

What he did during our Super Bowl season was one of the best coaching jobs I have ever seen in the NFL, and really in all sports. The number-one thing he did was create a strong culture within the team where the players owned the decisions and every detail. That brought the team together. He had a perfect balance of not coaching like a dictator, but also not letting the players take too much control either. He formed a partnership. That was probably the most impressive thing. His willingness to listen and ability to communicate made it all possible. Right from the beginning, he had a dynamic plan for the offense. Along with Frank Reich, John DeFilippo, and the offensive staff, he was able to develop Carson and manage the quarterback position with both Carson and Nick Foles. He was willing to take risks when it was smart. He listened to the analytics people when they told him what gave us the best chance to win. His ability to trust his support staff was huge.

When you are a great listener and a great communicator—and you combine that with being smart, focused, and unselfish—you can go very far. Coach Pederson treats everybody with respect and relates well with everyone in the building, from coaches to players to staff. We have a great situation here with an excellent young team and a talented young quarterback. So I think the future is very bright for Doug, and I'm looking forward to the next chapter.

Jeffrey Lurie, owner of the Philadelphia Eagles

CHAPTER 1

I'M GOING TO KICK YOUR TAIL

I worked my way through the sea of people on the sidelines at U.S. Bank Stadium until I reached the field, where that big white border provides sanctuary. Finally, the Super Bowl. All of my time in the NFL—fourteen years as a quarterback, two years as an offensive quality-control coach, two years as a quarterbacks coach, three years as an offensive coordinator, and two years as a head coach—had prepared me for this day.

I spotted New England Patriots head coach Bill Belichick down on the other end of the field. Eventually we connected at midfield and had a chance to say hello. I had met him at league meetings, but we'd never really had any conversation before this.

He congratulated me on the season and said it was great to be in this game. I said the same thing right back to him. Then he complimented our team and said, "I went back and tried to find some games you were losing in; I couldn't find many." I told him there were plenty of times.

But as much respect as I had for him, I was looking at him thinking of all the hard work it took to get to the Super Bowl, and all the doubters and naysayers who said our season was over after we lost our franchise quarterback. I was thinking of the sacrifice of long hours by my coaching staff. I was thinking of the players who committed to taking ownership. And then I thought the Patriots had no idea what the championship was about to them. I looked at him and thought, "I'm going to kick your tail, definitely going to kick your tail."

Everyone thinks I'm this soft-spoken, nice guy, but I have a highly competitive nature and an underdog mentality. I probably learned that underdog mentality being around people like Andy Reid, Brett Favre, and Dan Marino. They are ultimate competitors, and when that whistle blows, all gloves are off. I walked away to tend to my team, and Coach Belichick went to do his thing. It was the calm before the storm.

It seemed like a long time since we had played our last game. We had started game planning for the Patriots thirteen days earlier, the day after we beat the Vikings in the NFC Championship Game. We put the entire game plan together early that week, and then had a normal few days of practice. We even put the pads on.

Then we headed to Minneapolis on Sunday, a day earlier than we had to. I texted four of our strong leaders—Carson Wentz, Malcolm Jenkins, Jason Kelce, and Nick Foles—and asked them if the guys were feeling a little tired. They said they were and suggested we not do anything on Sunday. I thought it made sense, so I gave them the day off. The players were grateful.

It was back to work on Monday. We had meetings and walk-throughs in a ballroom at the hotel so they could get up and moving again. That night, the NFL kicked off Super Bowl week. It was a big media event with both teams at the event, and we all fielded questions. It was important to get back to routine, so I didn't change the schedule and treated Tuesday like a normal in-season day. We had meetings, did walk-throughs, everything as usual.

I did, though, give them enough time to enjoy the Mall of America and the NFL Experience and to see the sights around town. When I went to the Super Bowl with Green Bay back-to-back years as a player in the nineties, that was something Mike Holmgren allowed us to do. He let us enjoy the whole week and check out the host cities. Some of the parties were late at night, so we couldn't attend those, but he allowed us to go out and show our faces. Some of our players had dinner with Patriots players, or they ran into them someplace and hung out. Maybe they weren't buddy-buddy with them, but they could talk and have a laugh. I don't have a problem with that. It's all part of the scene.

On Wednesday, we had more meetings at the hotel, then took a bus to the University of Minnesota for practice. Jim Schwartz, our defensive coordinator, had been to a Super Bowl with the Tennessee Titans, and he recommended not putting in the whole game plan the first week. So the coaches and I saved about 10 percent of the game plan to put in that first week. This way it kept the players' minds engaged as we headed into the game.

We analyzed third down, red zone, two minute, four minute, fourth and goal, fourth and one, all those situations, so there was tweaking all week. We took eight or nine plays out and replaced them with those we had run earlier in the season, thinking that they would be more effective. Even though the players were familiar with the plays, reinstalling them in Minneapolis kept things from getting stale, especially for the quarterbacks.

During the season, I usually spend most of the week

leading up to a game in the quarterback meetings, but having the two weeks to prepare gave me the freedom to sit in on other position meetings. I sat in with my o-line and defensive units. It was important for the players to see me there, especially the defensive guys, whether it was in the rooms or during practice at their end of the field. As much as possible, I wanted to work with all the players.

I also called around for advice. More than anyone else, Andy Reid has helped me develop as a coach. We were together in Green Bay, Philadelphia, and Kansas City. He had Super Bowl experience, coaching the Eagles against the Patriots in Jacksonville. Among the things we talked about was preparing the team for all the downtime in the pregame and at halftime. That was interesting, and not something I had thought of.

Halftime during the Super Bowl is thirty minutes, as opposed to twelve minutes during the regular season. So during our Wednesday practice, I stopped it to take a thirty-minute time-out, simulating halftime in the locker room. I told the players to get off their feet and refuel and recharge, and the coaches to do their thing with game-plan adjustments and then to regroup with their units. Then we returned to the field and finished up practice. Some of the guys complained about their day being extended, but they got over it when they understood the reasoning.

Some players are able to take their games to the next level when the stakes are raised. Alshon Jeffery probably had his best week of practice all year. Nobody noticed it, but it was a big deal to us. I talked to Mike Groh, who was our wide receivers coach at the time, about how Alshon was practicing better and playing faster. He was showing up and paying attention to the details. He wasn't making any mental mistakes either, and he brought a positive attitude, talking up and cheering on his teammates.

We were excited to see what Alshon would do in the game. New England was a single-high coverage team, and they liked to go bump and run, and press. We knew Stephon Gilmore was going to be on him all day. Gilmore and Alshon were teammates and roommates at South Carolina, and Alshon was in Stephon's wedding party. So they knew each other pretty well. Gilmore can be a physical cornerback, so there was going to be contact. We didn't mind because Alshon's a big, tough guy. We tried to imitate that physical style in practice. Alshon was able to release at the line of scrimmage, get to the top of his route, get physical, and run that dagger route, which is one of Nick Foles's favorites. While we had seen Alshon nail it in games from time to time, we had never seen him do it so well in practice. On Thursday, he also ran some nice slants, which is one of the routes he likes to run. We have some third-down plays for when the defense is in man coverage; that week, we worked some combinations with Alshon, and again he was flawless, with Nick hitting him on time.

Then on Friday, which is red-zone day, Alshon really perked up. We had a quick fade route where he leaned on the corner, hit his stride, and Nick threw a ball that was a little high. To see him time and elevate his jump over the top of Sidney Jones was one of those "wow" moments. Sidney is going to be a good player for us, and he played the technique as best as he could, but Nick put the ball where only Alshon was going to get it. It was another one of those times when you knew this guy was in the zone and focused. I couldn't wait to see him go against Gilmore in the game and watch everything unfold.

Of course early in the Super Bowl, Alshon made that great catch in the back of the end zone for a touchdown. He had a great game with three catches for seventy-three yards, and made some big plays for us. What we saw in practice carried over into the game. He stood out.

It wasn't just Alshon. Nelson Agholor had a good week too. And the offensive line as a unit was executing really well. I hadn't seen that type of speed from our offense all year in practice. Maybe it was because of the big game and emotions were running high. The defense was the same way, with the defensive line rolling off the ball, linebackers flying, and the secondary making plays on the ball. I saw the timing, the pass rush. Fletcher Cox and Derek Barnett with their moves, Chris Long showing off his power and quickness. Those things were flashing. In the grind of the season, sometimes you're just trying to get through the practice. But here, when it mattered most, the team put together some of the best practices I'd seen in a long while.

The two weeks weren't perfect, though. Far from it. I bet we had a total of a dozen players and coaches, myself included, who were sick. The flu, or flulike symptoms, was running rampant in our team. I was sick right after the Minnesota game and had it for four days. I still wasn't feeling well the first couple of days in Minneapolis, with chills, body aches, and a fever of 100.6 degrees. I took a flu test along with a bunch of the other guys, and mine was negative. But the bug was going around. Jim Schwartz had it twice. Duce Staley, my running backs coach, had it. Nelson Agholor fell sick on Thursday before the game. Tim Jernigan couldn't practice Wednesday or Thursday and stayed back at the hotel. Player after player, coach after coach. All I could think was, "Oh boy, great, this is what we need, everyone getting sick with the biggest game of our careers—of our lives—coming up."

We had a good time away from football too. My wife, Jeannie, flew out with me, and the kids came out later in the week. Friday night was fun: the Eagles rented out the Hard Rock Cafe in the Mall of America. We had a real entourage: my mom; Jeannie; our three boys—Drew, who was twenty-three, Josh, twenty, and Joel, fifteen; Drew's girlfriend, Ann Marie; my sister, Cathy; Jeannie's two brothers and their wives; and family friends from New Jersey and Kansas. We had about twenty of us at the party. Our head of security, Dom DiSandro, hung around with us for precautionary reasons. We had a private area for Eagles family and friends where drinks and appetizers were served. When friends of the team are involved, they often want to get autographs or pictures, so we went to this cove where we were tucked away. There was a band and everyone was having fun.

The Mall of America is so huge that it holds an amusement park, Nickelodeon Universe, and the boys, of course, told me I needed to ride on the roller coasters with them. I love roller coasters. "You're an NFL head coach and it's the Friday before the Super Bowl," I thought. "You're supposed to represent the Philadelphia Eagles and set an example." And then I said to myself, "Let's go. What the heck!"

Avatar Airbender was my favorite. I rode that and Rock Bottom Plunge three times. And then I rode Fairly Odd Coaster twice. They let us stay a little later for a couple more rides after they shut down at 10:00. It was fun to enjoy the moment with the boys. I came back to the party, and

Dom asked where I'd gone. I said, "Dude, you gotta come on this ride!" He was shocked.

Before the NFC Championship Game, Brett Favre told me if we made it to the Super Bowl he'd be glad to talk to the team. Brett and I played together for the Packers for eight years and became very close. I told him I would hold him to it. So on Saturday morning, he came by the hotel to speak to the guys. It was supposed to be a surprise, but there are spies everywhere. Things got out, and the next thing I knew one of the players said, "Hey, I hear you're having Brett Favre come talk to us." Oh well.

Brett spoke for about ten minutes, sharing the importance of knowing the opponent. He said we needed to be aware that the Patriots understood what a Super Bowl was like and that they could control their emotions better as a result. He told some stories about our Packers team in our first Super Bowl, how we were juiced up and emotional. Yet we needed to learn how to deal with the long stretches of time when we wouldn't be playing. As big a stage as the Super Bowl is, there's so much time at pregame, so much time at halftime, and so much downtime in the couple of weeks leading up to it. He put it all into perspective for the guys.

After he finished, I said a couple of words to the team before we went about our day. Then I closed by saying, "We will win this game."

I had been saying that to the team every day since the postseason began. It wasn't, "We will do everything we can to win this game." It was, "We will win this game." I thought if I said it enough, we would believe it. We felt we would win our games as the season went along, but I never verbalized it before the playoffs. While we believed we were a better team in most of our games, anything can happen in the postseason. I needed something to give them the confidence. After all, people weren't giving us the respect that we had earned. We were the number-one seed in the NFC, with home-field advantage throughout the playoffs, and we had defeated the Atlanta Falcons, the previous year's NFC champions, we had beaten the Minnesota Vikings, the league's number-one defense, and now we were in the Super Bowl. Yet there were those who felt we didn't belong on the same field as the Patriots.

I can honestly say by the time I was standing on U.S. Bank Field, I had no doubts that we would win. I had watched a lot of tape, including the previous year's Super Bowl when the Patriots came back against the Falcons. In fact, I reviewed a lot of games where the Patriots were losing and came back, focusing on their ability to pull it off. What did I learn? It wasn't about the Patriots as much as it was about the teams they were playing. Their opponents weren't playing for sixty minutes. They weren't finishing.

They weren't executing their offense. Play callers became more conservative and stopped being aggressive.

A great example was the AFC Championship Game. When the Jacksonville Jaguars had a four-point lead on New England and had the ball with fifty-five seconds left in the first half, they took a knee and ran the clock out. I was watching the game from our locker room at Lincoln Financial Field as we were getting ready to play Minnesota. I sat there thinking, "You have got to be kidding me right now." They had two time-outs and close to a minute left. They could have at least tried for a field goal. They took it out of their quarterback's hands, and they didn't give it to their big back, Leonard Fournette. I thought, "If they lose this game, this is why." Sure enough, they would go on to lose the game.

It made me mad because Jacksonville had New England right where they wanted them. I was screaming at the television in my office. When they knelt right before halftime, inside I was like, "I'll never do that." It fueled me. Against the Vikings later that day, we had twenty-nine seconds left in the first half and three time-outs. Instead of taking a knee, I called for a screen pass to Jay Ajayi to the sideline, a pass to Zach Ertz up the sideline, another pass to Ajayi, and then we kicked a field goal to grab three points. All in twenty-nine seconds. That's how I wanted to play the last minute of a half—with an aggressive mentality.

So as we prepared for the Super Bowl, I told my guys, "Let's talk about this New England mystique. There is no such thing. If we play for sixty minutes, if we own our jobs, if we do the things we're supposed to do, play error-free, play mistake-free, play loose, play passionate, all the things you've done all season, we're going to win this game. I'm speaking to myself and I'm speaking to everyone in this room—we will win this game. There's no mystique in New England. Tom Brady is a great quarterback, one of the greatest of all time. Bill Belichick will be in the Hall of Fame; he's a great coach. These two together have won a lot of championships, and I respect that. As a former player and as a coach, I respect that because that's what we all strive to do. We all want the five, six, seven titles. We want to be in this game every year. But it's not about mystique; it's not about Tom Brady. The teams they played just quit; they shut down."

The night before the Super Bowl, I slept like a baby, going to bed a little after 11:00 and waking up around 8:00, feeling confident and calm.

At the stadium, my two older sons, Drew and Josh, were on the field with me, and they would stay on the sideline during the game. For me as a dad it was cool seeing them out there Snapchatting, taking selfies and pictures, and all of that. They had joined me on the field before during regular season games, but in this environment, it was a first. I wanted them to enjoy it with me. Who knows if you're going to get back out there ever again?

Then it was back in the locker room as the game grew near. At this point, I felt the knot in the pit of my stomach. Truth be told, if you don't get nervous for a game like this, you're not normal. But this was more nervous than I had ever felt. It was overwhelming. I thought, "Man, I'm in the freaking Super Bowl." I wanted to pinch myself.

Once the ball was in the air, it was all about the game. We took a 9–3 lead on Alshon's touchdown. Then LeGarrette Blount had a big run for a touchdown to put us up by twelve. You talk about a guy that's been to two Super Bowls with the Patriots, an unselfish player, who had a big role in creating our success this season—that's LeGarrette. He stood next to me during the game. He kept saying over and over, "They can't beat us. They can't beat us." I'd tell him he was right. To me, having exchanges like that, as brief as they are, in the biggest game of our careers, said something. You could hear the players on the sidelines go, "Let's just keep it moving, we're in a good spot, and we're going to be fine." People didn't read about these conversations, but as the head coach, hearing these words made it special. It's the culture I've established that they believe in themselves, and that they trust in each other.

In the course of our preparations, I asked LeGarrette

and Chris Long, our former Patriots, about Belichick and what to expect. "You're going to have to make adjustments at halftime," they said. "He's going to adjust, so you're going to have to adjust. He's a smart coach; he's intellectual." He really does make adjustments. If you watch games, he takes over in the second half. It could be a terrible first half, but in the second half they catch their stride on both sides of the ball. LeGarrette and Chris wanted to avoid talking about him too much, though. They wanted this to be about us and what *we* did. That was the other message. They said, "Who cares what he does? Let's go win the game. This is about us. Let's go win this game for *us*."

With thirty-eight seconds left in the first half, we ran a play called Philly Special that helped us do just that. Press Taylor, who was my offensive quality-control at the time, is responsible for reviewing NFL games and college games and looking for special gadget–type plays. When we see a good one, we save it and put it in a folder.

In 2016, the Chicago Bears used the play on a third down against the Vikings at the two-yard line. They executed it perfectly. I said, "That's the play that's going to win us a game." I just had to find where we would put it in. We had Trey Burton, a University of Florida baseball guy and a former high school quarterback who was a third tight end for us and who played a lot. He could throw. And we had Corey

Clement, an undrafted rookie running back who we used in the red zone. He'd be with Nick Foles in the backfield.

The week of the NFC Championship Game, I thought we needed something extra, so I reviewed the folder for special gadget plays and added Philly Special to the red-zone game plan. Since it was a new play, I wanted to get as many reps in as possible, so we practiced it during our walk-through Thursday and ran it again live in practice on Friday.

The first time we did it, Trey threw a heat-seeking missile to Nick. That wasn't going to work. "Trey, you can't throw it that hard," I advised him. "Throw a grenade to him. Just float it to him and let it come down in his hands." We ran it again and then he overthrew it, sailed it five yards over Nick's head. At that point I said, "Okay, got it, let's move on to the next play. I don't think I'll be calling this."

Still, even though we had yet to get past the Vikings, Nick Foles and I would occasionally talk about the play. "How cool would it be if I call Philly Special and it's the game winner in the Super Bowl?" But then I reconsidered. "No, if I call it, it's going to be the game winner against Minnesota." As it turned out, we never used it in that game because the situation didn't come up.

When we built the game plan for the Super Bowl, Frank Reich, my offensive coordinator, and I looked over the plays we didn't use in the NFC Championship Game that we could carry over to the Super Bowl. Philly Special was one of them. We now had a couple of weeks to look at the play on film, look at our practice tape, work adjustments, and make corrections. We had to iron out the verbiage, the cadence, and a lot of other things. But as coaches we are often paranoid, especially when we are being watched as closely as we were during Super Bowl week. You never know who is watching practice, and we didn't want it to be talked about publicly. So we didn't rep it the entire week at practice. We did review it a couple of times at the hotel, in walk-throughs, and watching it on film.

Now, back to the game. There are thirty-four seconds left in the first half, and we are fourth and goal at the one-yard line. I told the team we were going for it, and then we took a time-out. I'm sure everybody watching thought I had changed my mind and had decided to attempt a field goal. But I hadn't. When Nick came over during the time-out, I was reviewing the red-zone, fourth-down, and two-point menus.

"How about Philly Philly?" he asked. That's what he called Philly Special. My eyes never hit on it because I planned on using it on the two- or three-yard line, not the one-yard line. I thought for a second and said, "You know what, let's do it."

I called the wristband number, 122 (Nick wore a

wristband on which each play was typed, corresponding to a number). I never verbalized the play, so none of my coaches knew I'd called it. LeGarrette Blount came up over my shoulder and whispered, "What do you got?" I pointed to the red-zone section of my call sheet and told him. Then John DeFilippo, our quarterbacks coach, called out the play and all the other coaches said, "Holy crap, it's Philly Special. It's Super Bowl time and it's Philly Special." Of course, the rest is history. Corey took the snap, pitched to Trey, and Trey threw a perfect pass to Nick, who was wide open for the touchdown that put us up 22–12.

You hear people say, "Man, that was the gutsiest call in Super Bowl history," and I just shrug. I trust my players. Nick made a suggestion, and I agreed to it. I could have just trumped it, but then again, earlier I was standing next to Bill Belichick at the fifty-yard line and thinking about how I was going to beat his tail. The play was awesome. It worked great.

Some have said that if the players didn't execute, I'd be on the street now, looking for a job. But I never thought about that. You can't. If I had, I wouldn't have called the play.

Since they knew what to expect after we rehearsed it on Wednesday, the guys were prepared for the longer halftime. Usually, with a twelve-minute halftime you're in and out, with barely enough time to sit, think, and go to the bathroom before you're right back out there for the second half.

When we first went into the locker room, I was in Mike Zimmer's office with the offensive staff, and we were rushing through everything and talking fast. I stepped in and said, "Time-out. We have thirty minutes to do this. Let's relax. Let's take a deep breath and go back through it." It was a little more civilized then. The players were able to recharge and prepare for the second half, which was good. We needed to enjoy the moment.

In the second half, the Patriots kept coming, as we figured they would. Thankfully, Nick threw a touchdown pass to Corey on our first possession of the third quarter to give us some breathing room.

One of the only mistakes Nick made in the game was calling the wrong play on a third-and-one play on what turned out to be the game-winning drive for us in the fourth quarter. I called wristband number 52. Nick looked at his wristband and mistakenly called the play that was right above it, 50. It was a play-action pass, which wasn't the right play.

We brought Torrey Smith in motion, then slid him back into the left flat. The defensive end hung, and didn't rush off the edge. Well, Torrey beat him, and Nick threw a dangerous lob pass over his head. Torrey caught it, but was tackled for no gain.

Nobody on the coaching staff even noticed Nick called the wrong play until after the game. I was already thinking about the next play, so I didn't even realize it. When they told me about it and I went back to look at it, I thought about how disastrous that could have been if the pass had been intercepted.

Nick was brilliant in the game. A lot of people on the outside thought he couldn't fill Carson Wentz's shoes and wondered if he could lead us to a championship. When we grade players, especially quarterbacks, it's based on decision-making—did he make the right read? And we look at timing and accuracy. In that game Nick was almost perfect in the way he executed the offense, as well as in his mentality. He was under control, yet he played as fearlessly in his decisions and throws as I tried to be with my play calls. His grade was the highest of any player on our team for the game. By far. It also was the highest of any player on our team for the season.

I'm sure it surprised some people. But it didn't surprise me. I knew Nick, so I had faith. Some of his teammates might not have felt as confident in him as I was. There was a percentage of guys who doubted because they didn't know him. But then there were a handful of guys who did know him. They thought, "We're going to be fine. Nick's going to be good. He's not a rookie, he's a veteran guy, he's going to do it." Some of the guys had played with Nick when he was here with Chip Kelly and Andy Reid. Brandon Graham, Fletcher Cox, Vinny Curry, Brent Celek, Jason Kelce, Jason Peters—all those guys were brought to Philly by Andy. So they knew Nick. They grew up with him, saw him have a Pro Bowl season with Chip. There was history.

Of course, Brady was playing incredibly as well. He gave the Patriots a one-point lead with a touchdown pass to Rob Gronkowski with a little more than nine minutes left. That's when things really got interesting.

Everyone talks about Philly Special. It was unique and creative. You can say it was a gutsy call on the goal line with time running out in the half. But to me, the more difficult decision to make was the fourth-and-one call on our own forty-five in the fourth quarter with 6:05 left in the game and the clock running. The whole season was hanging on that play. If we didn't get it, we would have given Brady a chance to go forty-five yards, and then if he scored, it probably would have been game over.

The play was designed to go to Zach Ertz, and it did. Nick was almost sacked on the play. Two guys came off the left edge and he had to sidestep both of them to deliver an accurate throw to Zach. It was a play we had previously run in the game, though with a different formation. We'd practiced it many times during the course of the year. We needed one yard and we got two. That allowed us to go down the field and then hit Ertz again for the score to take a 38–33 lead.

I made that fourth-down call because I didn't want to put the ball back in Tom's hands if we didn't have to. I wanted to continue to be aggressive in play calling. I felt really good about the call at the time, and still do. Nobody said much about it, but if there is a play from the Super Bowl that I was proud of, it was that one. It was big.

The only time I became nervous was after we took that five-point lead and we gave them the ball back with a little more than two minutes remaining. I went down by the defense and said, "Everything you got, guys. Everything you got, every single play." Our guys were not buying into the New England mystique at that point. What they bought into was something else I had been preaching—we had to play for sixty minutes against this team. Regardless of what happened in the first fifty-eight minutes, we had to play for sixty. We had to do our jobs better at the end of the game, become more focused, become more poised.

It applied to me too. For the previous ten days or so, all I heard were comparisons between me and Bill Belichick. It was, "How can Doug Pederson outcoach the great Bill Belichick?" They said I was going to be so overmatched, so overpowered, so overwhelmed. I knew what it was about, but I went into the game trusting my guys and myself. "I've done it this way the entire season," I thought. "Why should I change for one game?"

If anything, I was more aggressive because I gave the Patriots the respect. You knew they were going to score touchdowns. You knew they were going to get it to Gronkowski. We had to score.

We gave up 613 yards. Tom threw for 505 yards—the most ever in a postseason game. But all we needed was one play, and we got it. Brandon Graham sacked Brady and forced a fumble, then Derek Barnett recovered. We kicked the field goal and went up by eight.

When Brady's last pass went up, it was like slow motion. I was hoping it would hit the ground. Gronkowski posted up, and it looked like he was going to grab it in the air, but the ball fell. Then it was mayhem, total freaking mayhem, a tornado on that field. They dumped Gatorade on me. Chris Wilson, my defensive line coach, and I embraced. Then the confetti flew. Everyone ran onto the field. People were running into one another; cameras were everywhere. Total chaos.

I was hugging players and trying to get through the crowd to find Bill Belichick. He congratulated me and wished me the best, and I did the same. They had a great season.

That celebration on the field was pretty special. Being there with my guys, hugging them, with the weight finally lifted. After a while I found my sons Drew and Josh. Drew said, "We're freaking World Champs!" That's a great memory. I found Jeannie and Joel, our youngest son. They had Philadelphia Eagles World Champs hats flying around the stadium. My family joined me on the podium. I was overwhelmed with emotion. I didn't know if I was going to cry, laugh, or both.

Then they walked the trophy down and it started to sink in. "Wow, we just won the Super Bowl." Our owner, Jeffrey Lurie, was up there with his family, and he was beside himself. Nick Foles and his wife and his baby were up there. So were Howie Roseman and his family, Carson Wentz, Zach Ertz, and our president, Don Smolenski. You shared that moment with everyone.

Dan Patrick hosted the ceremony, and when I had a chance to address the fans and hoist up the trophy for the first time, it was incredible. Afterward, the media converged on me. Every microphone and camera was in my face to the point where I was feeling claustrophobic. Sal Paolantonio grabbed me right away and we did a quick interview for ESPN. The whole time, I was wondering when I would speak to the team. We usually talk right after the game, but in this environment I didn't know when I would have the chance. I started thinking about that, about when the buses were going to leave for the party, and about a bunch of other things because coaches are always on schedules. I finally told myself to relax and enjoy this.

Eventually, I left the field and knocked out the press conference. Finally, I was able to get into the dressing room for the first time. The team was going nuts. They were dancing and taking videos with their cell phones, and some media people were there. It was long after the game now, but I still had to talk to them. I spoke about the journey that brought us here, and how we won, about the emotion that went into it. All the little things I harped on all season long had paid off.

The buses started heading over to the party for all the Eagles and our families and friends. We didn't get there until around 11:00. I had twenty-two guests, and there were about two thousand people there. The place was packed. That's when the relief hit. The hard part was over. Some of the players who I didn't see after the game came up to me with joy on their faces.

The song "Dreams and Nightmares" came on. The song is by Meek Mill, a Philadelphia rapper who our guys have taken a liking to. I looked up, and the entire team was up on the stage with the Super Bowl trophy, dancing to the song. I said to Jeannie, "I have to go up there." I snaked my way through the crowd. When I got to the middle of the stage with the trophy, the guys were yelling, "Coach!" and I was jumping up and down with them, having a good time.

The whole thing was surreal. I was asking myself, "What did we just do?" The accomplishment still hadn't sunk in.

The next day, there was a lot of talk about being fearless. I appreciate that, obviously. But it was about more than that. It was about the trust I'd been talking about, and relationships built with the players and the coaches and the staff. It was about coaching up guys hard every day, getting them to practice. All of that makes those calls on game days— those gutsy calls—pretty easy to make. Once you study it, you know the situation is right, and you trust your guys, it's easy to be fearless.

The way I look at it: if I only get one opportunity to do this in my life, I'm going to go down swinging. If I never get back here again, at least I can say that I gave it my best shot. I didn't want to hold anything back. I'm not playing next week; there's no next game.

Some of the fans around town have come up to me and said, "They're going to knock down the Rocky Balboa statue by the Philadelphia Museum of Art and put up a statue of you."

I laugh and say, "No, you can't knock down Rocky. He's the pride of Philadelphia. But I can relate to him."

CHAPTER 2

RISK-TAKER

I'm not a guy who enjoys going to the casino, and I don't gamble. My wife, Jeannie, and I are also pretty conservative investors with a balanced portfolio of mutual funds. When it comes to football, though, it's a different story. I'm considered a high-risk play caller. I'm fine with that. I didn't sign up to be average. I want to be great in this business and leave my mark on young players' lives and on our organization. Forget the status quo.

Our owner, Jeffrey Lurie, talks about being risk-takers, putting ourselves out there and taking chances. So I'm going to push the envelope. I'll tell my team during a meeting, "I'm asking you to give me everything this Sunday." But it doesn't end there. "You're getting my best on Sunday too," I'll add. "I'm going to stay aggressive and so are our other coaches. We'll put you in position to attack."

Coaching that way sends a message to the team. It shows the level of confidence that I have in the guys. When I go for it on fourth down, it not only shows confidence in the offense, but it also signals to the defense that if we don't get the first down, I trust them to stop the opponent and get the ball back. By the way, it puts the other team on notice too.

If you keep coaching that way, it becomes a mind-set: the way you do anything is the way you should do everything. So you operate with an aggressive mentality all the time. That's what we created. It's a little bit of a monster, but it's a good monster.

I picked Andy Reid's brain about this when I was an assistant for him, wondering why he called certain things. The way he sees it is after you get a chunk play—twenty yards or more—there are two ways you can go. You can either call a nice, conservative play, or you can take a shot. So each week, I identify the area of the field—between certain yard lines—where I will take a shot. And then I won't bat an eye when the opportunity comes.

We went for it on fourth down twenty-six times in 2017. That was the second-most in the NFL. The opposing team knows that they will have to defend us on all four downs. If we cross the fifty-yard line, you better know we're in four-down territory. More often than not, if we have a fourth down inside the five-yard line, we will go for it.

Our players love it. Guys like Jason Peters and Jason Kelce have come up to me during games and said things like "Great call" and "Appreciate the confidence." That means something to me.

Now that I have established that approach to fourth down, they not only expect it, they want it. When I started out as a head coach, they had no idea. The offense would run off the field thinking we were punting, and I'd say, "Nope, we're going for it on fourth down." Now they know the situations when they will stay on the field. They're actually mad when we punt the ball, and I get some grief, usually from the offensive linemen. With the offense's expectations, I might go for it all the time, but I have to be careful. Kevin Kelley, the head coach at Pulaski Academy in Arkansas, almost never punts regardless of where he is on the field. I don't think I'll be following his lead, though.

For us, it's always a calculated risk. If it leads to more wins for the Philadelphia Eagles, I'm going to take it. If the numbers back me up on that, then it's my job to find ways of putting our team in position to make the first downs.

The decision is based on a number of variables. How well

are we playing offense? How well are we playing defense? What is our field position and distance for a first down or touchdown? Who is the opponent? You have to look at the big picture, not just pieces of it. I'm processing that information with my coaches before and during the game.

The decision-making process for a fourth down starts on third down. Ryan Paganetti, our defensive quality-control coach, helps me with these decisions from his seat in the press box. He manages the fourth-down, two-point, and time-out charts. He might say, "If you could get it to fourth and one, the numbers say we go for it." The coaches rehearse these scenarios on Saturdays prior to game so we don't have to do a lot of guesswork. We don't have a lot of time to process in a game, and I don't like to guess. If you guess too much, you will lose.

At the end of the day, it's my decision to pull the trigger on whether or not to go for it. After all, I'm putting our team at risk. If we don't make it, the opposing team has the ball with great field position and with a chance for a field goal and maybe a touchdown. If they score, everyone says it's because of my call.

Some might think I make these calls with my gut. That's a part of it. There are times when I ignore the numbers. Maybe we're in a six-, seven-, eight-play drive and we're moving the ball. I don't care what the numbers say then. At that point, if the gut says go for it, I'm in.

My first instinct usually is the right one. I don't second-guess it, but trust it. That was the message in Malcolm Gladwell's book *Blink*. I used to tell Andy Reid this quite a bit when he was calling offensive plays for us in Kansas City. There would be a decision on third down to make and he'd ask me if I liked this play or that play. I'd say, "Coach, go with your gut. Go with the first play you thought of." Andy usually agreed.

Through my time in the league I've heard plenty of players and coaches say, "I should have trusted my gut." There were times in 2017 when I'd be caught between two plays and Frank Reich would sound like me advising Andy—"Trust your instincts," he'd say. And sure enough, it was the right play in most cases. I was fortunate to have Frank as my coordinator for my first two seasons with the Eagles.

One that was a true gut call was a fourth and one against the Rams out in Los Angeles last December. It was in the second quarter. We were on the Rams' thirty-one-yard line. We had a play on third down that got us to fourth and one. I didn't even consider the numbers or probability. We had already scored fourteen points and were moving the ball pretty well. My gut said we were going to roll, so we got in our quick-tempo offense. Carson Wentz hit Nelson Agholor in the flat, and Nelson just turned it up down the sideline to the thirteen-yard line. That was just going off instinct.

The play, by the way, wasn't even in the game plan that week. We had practiced it in training camp, so the players remembered it well enough to execute it. It ended up being perfect for the situation, and Trey Burton scored three plays later.

But it doesn't always work out like that. I was criticized for a fourth-down call in September against the Giants. We had crossed midfield. I thought it was fourth and seven, though we later found out it was more like fourth and eight, and one yard can make a difference in these decisions. In that situation, the numbers were more favorable to punt the ball and vie for field position. I elected to go for it, Carson was sacked, and we gave the Giants a short field. They drove the ball to the two, and a pass from Eli Manning to Sterling Shepard was ruled a touchdown. Fortunately, though, it was overruled on replay. After Manning threw an incompletion, we stopped them on fourth down. So we got away with one.

I am becoming known for going for two-point conversions. In 2017, we attempted two-point conversions nine times—the most in the league. We converted six of them—the most in the league. No other team had more than three.

Our conversion percentage of .667 was the best among the teams that had more than two attempts.

To decide whether to kick an extra point or attempt a two-point conversion, I study our opponent. I look at how well their goal-line defense is playing. I consider this—eight points look worse than seven to the opponent. I learned this from Mike Tomlin. I don't know Mike well, but I've noticed from afar that Pittsburgh goes for two quite a bit. They often attempt two-point conversions in the first half, mainly in the first quarter. These attempts create a competitive and psychological advantage.

Sometimes it's just about scoring as many points as we can, so two-point conversion decisions are driven a little more by emotions. For instance, in 2017, when we played the Panthers we lined up at the fifteen-yard line for the extra point and there was a defensive penalty. We made the kick and could've kept the point, but I said, "Forget it, we're going for two." You can look at it like you are taking a point off the board, or you are adding one. I believe in the latter, not the former. Of course, you have to convert, but I don't worry about that.

Former Eagles wide receiver Vince Papale loaned me a book, *The Navy SEAL Art of War* by Rob Roy. It's about some great principles Roy learned through his SEAL experiences. He writes about standing in front of a group and asking,

"Right now, how many pushups can you do?" When people answer with a number of pushups, say, twenty-five, he says, "Why would you limit yourself to just twenty-five? Why not think bigger and give yourself a chance to do more?" So one of the things I took from that book is that there is no benefit to putting ourselves in a box. Let's expand our boundaries, think bigger. Let's not play it safe and then have regrets. I talk to my coaches about it all the time.

A lot of NFL coaches have traditionally been averse to taking risks. Even some of the coaches on my staff have had to adjust to our aggressive approach. In my first year with the Eagles, in a game against the Vikings, there were fifteen seconds left in the first half and we had a second down on the seventeen-yard line. We had a five-point lead. Some of my offensive coaches were advising me to kick the field goal then and there. I wanted to take a shot to the end zone first, then kick the field goal.

Even if we threw it away, a play would waste only five or six seconds and we still would have time on third down to kick the field goal. We didn't execute the play, and we eventually settled for the field goal anyway. Still, we wasted time off the clock and gave the ball back to the Vikings without enough time for them to score. I didn't want them to have a chance for a return, a big play, or a pass interference.

Afterward, the coaches all said they loved it, and they changed their tune.

The rest of the league has noticed how we do things. I had two coaches that left me after the Super Bowl. John DeFilippo became the offensive coordinator for Minnesota and Frank Reich became the head coach in Indianapolis. Both of them said, "Coach, appreciate everything, but the biggest takeaway is that I'm going to maintain the aggressive play calling." They were grateful for what they learned in two years with me. They also talked about how they came to understand the value of trusting—trusting their players, trusting their instincts, and trusting their commitment to stay aggressive.

At the NFL scouting combine in Indianapolis in March, I was talking with Rams coach Sean McVay, and he was asking about Xs and Os in general—not necessarily the play calling, but some of the play designs and our use of personnel. We talked about that aggressive style and putting our players in positions to be successful to maintain an edge.

Coaches watch each other's game films to see what we can learn from them. With the Rams, you had one of the top-scoring offenses in the National Football League in 2017. I found what the Rams did interesting because they seemed very simplistic in the sense that they ran a lot of the same plays over and over, but they used different personnel groupings, formations, motions, and shifts.

Jon Gruden also came up to me. He said, "Those were some ballsy calls in the Super Bowl, man, on the biggest stage. There's not many people that make those calls, if any." Coming from him, someone who has coached and called plays in the National Football League and won a Super Bowl, that's a compliment. Arizona offensive coordinator Mike McCoy said some nice things, too, how he appreciated our use of offensive personnel. These coaches understood our aggressive nature and how we trusted the players. When it comes from your peers, it really means something.

It's important for coaches to study game management too. We have to put in the time during the week so we are prepared on game day. Fourth downs, two-point conversions, sometimes a call on third down, when to use time-outs, when to use challenge flags, two-minute drives—those calls can win or lose games. Think about our NFC Championship Game. We had twenty-nine seconds and three time-outs before the half. We continued to attack, went down, and kicked a field goal right before time expired. If we didn't study those situations and prepare, none of that would have happened.

Some coaches don't want to spend time studying those scenarios, but as you can tell, I believe it's important. Bill Belichick is prepared. He and his staff are studying their opponent and every situation so that on game day they have that competitive advantage to make quick decisions.

This applies to challenge flags too. If I'm not rehearsing what to challenge and what not to challenge, we're in trouble. I need someone in my ear that's helping me make that decision. It takes the whole staff to get the job done. Needless to say, it's not all about me. In this case, Jon Ferrari, our director of football compliance, helps me with the calls. He has a monitor in the press box, so he watches the game feeds and TV coverage, which we don't have access to down on the field. I always tell him, "Don't guess." It's either a yes or a no. It's either going to cost me a time-out and field position, or it's going to gain us field position and save the time-out if we're successful.

Jon did a great job communicating with me after watching the film. We challenged seven calls in the 2017 season and had three overturned. It's a collaborative effort for us. While I don't know if every team has those pieces, if you're not studying those situations and managing that element of the game, you are spinning your wheels.

With Howie Roseman as the general manager, our team has been bold off the field with personnel moves. Trading Sam Bradford to the Vikings before the 2016 season for first- and fourth-round picks was very risky. It was probably the biggest risk of my coaching career, which hadn't even gotten off the ground. Sam was going into the season as our starter, and with our first game a little more than one week away, he was gone. I had told the media that Sam was my guy and that our rookie Carson Wentz was our third quarterback and would sit a year. Chase Daniel, our other veteran quarterback, was our number two.

I was on board with this trade, though. Howie and I discuss big decisions, and I was willing to take on the challenge. I had thought a lot about it. We had drafted Carson to be our future. Now we were on the brink of the 2016 regular season and we had a decision to make. Do we trade our starter, a veteran quarterback in this league, and start a rookie who's never played and has missed most of the preseason with cracked ribs? Are we really going into the season with a rookie starting quarterback? Even Jeannie told me I was committing career suicide. After I processed the whole thing, I said, "You know what? Rookie coach. Rookie quarterback. New team. Why not? If we're going to do this, let's do it from day one. Let's not wait until year two or year three." We might have been a better team with Sam in the short term, but the trade enabled us to be a better team in the long term.

So I told Howie I was comfortable with the move. Then came all the scrutiny. A lot of articles were written about how crazy we were. They said a new head coach would have to explain the decision to go with a rookie quarterback to a veteran locker room, and everyone would look at me like, "What are you doing, Coach?" So I had to deal with media second-guessing.

Once we made the trade, the first person I called was Sam. It was a tough call to make. I thanked him for everything he had done and wished him well. His initial response was shock and disbelief, but as we talked through it, he understood and said he was looking forward to the opportunity. Then I called Carson and told him he was starting week one. I asked him how he felt about it. All he said was, "Let's go, let's go!" He was fired up and excited.

Chase was next. I'd been in his shoes before as a quarterback. I told him if he was going to get mad, get mad at me because it was my call. I wanted him to fully understand where we were taking the organization and that Carson was drafted for a reason. After we traded Sam, I could have started Chase, whom I brought from Kansas City to be the veteran backup. After all, Carson was still learning.

Chase was awesome about it, though. He fully supported Carson and was a big help, showing him how and what to study. He helped Carson divvy up his weekly workload, going through first and second down with him on Wednesday, red zone on Thursday, and then goal line and short yardage on Friday.

There were some other risky moves prior to the season. One of our first offseason signings was Alshon Jeffery, who hadn't been 100 percent healthy for a couple of seasons with the Chicago Bears. So it was fair to ask if we were gaining a player who would be available for a full sixteen games. From the outside, there was a perception that he wasn't happy— maybe there was a riff with the Bears coaching staff, or he wasn't getting the ball enough for his liking. Those were some of the questions we had to have answered before we signed him.

We found out he's unbelievable. He's a great team player who works hard. Maybe when he's not feeling great he doesn't want to go 100 percent in practice. He wants to go 75 percent or 70 percent. We had him work with our sports science, medical, and nutritional teams—anything we could do to help him stay healthy. And he played every game in 2017. Our perspective on him totally changed after he walked in the door.

That same offseason we signed LeGarrette Blount. He had an off-the-field incident in 2014 when he was with the

Steelers. There were also a couple of things that popped up in New England with people saying he was a bad guy and bad teammate. When he came to Philadelphia, people said the media would eat us both alive. But there was never one issue. Not one. So we avoided what everyone on the outside said was going to be an issue.

Then during the season, Jay Ajayi wore out his welcome in Miami. I don't know what happened down there, but I do know the coach didn't want him anymore. He was a bad egg, a bad apple, a cancer in the locker room, or whatever they were calling him. We traded for him, taking that gamble because of his talent level. What helped us was that by that point we had established our culture and we were winning some games. He came here, and again, we had no problems. Another potential issue avoided.

It was no different from when I was a player with the Packers. When we made that run for our first Super Bowl, Ron Wolf and Mike Holmgren brought in Andre Rison. He was also known as Bad Moon Rison. He was a disgruntled Atlanta Falcon who wore out his welcome. Then he went to the Browns, then the Jaguars. They said he had a bad attitude on the field, that he was picking fights and wasn't a team player. Well, he came to Green Bay, and he was perfect and helped us win a Super Bowl.

A big part of it is the culture takes over. Rison was put in an environment where he didn't want to be the reason that his team would lose. His teammates had a good thing going. His attitude was, "I don't want to be the guy to screw it up." That's what culture can do.

In those days, there was no question that watching Brett Favre play gave me a greater appreciation of taking risks. He was a true gunslinger and someone who did whatever it took to win the game. He dropped back and threaded the needle when his receiver was covered by two guys, and he somehow fit the ball in there. Watching him shaped my philosophy— don't worry about tomorrow; let's figure out how to do this today.

It's true he threw a lot of interceptions, but the thing is, he didn't care. He believed he would beat you. He might throw three picks but would throw four touchdowns, including the one that would beat you at the end of the game. And that's how I approached things as the season went on. I'm not worrying about tomorrow, man—let's figure out how to win this game today. If it means making some tough decisions or calls that are unconventional, I'm okay with that.

I didn't play quarterback with the same mentality Brett did. I didn't have the athleticism or arm strength to do that. I had to be a little more controlled and calculated in my play, and in the level of risk I took.

*　　*　　*

When I was at Ferndale High School, I started both ways, at quarterback and free safety. I've always been a quarterback at heart, but I loved defense too. I loved to hit and tackle. The gamble was whether to go for the interception or for that tackle and give up a completion.

Off the field, I did some things I shouldn't have when I was a kid. I grew up in Ferndale, Washington, which is a great place. It's a farming area. The big industry there is the refineries on Puget Sound. And it's surrounded by the spectacular Cascade mountain range.

Our neighbors had a well. It wasn't made of cinderblocks or bricks, and I didn't have to climb to get into it. It basically was a hole in the ground that was filled with water. I was about eight or nine years old and was curious about it and I took off the cover and looked down into it. I got too close and slipped on the grass and fell in. I was treading water in the well all by myself; no one around. I was pretty scared and yelled for help. The grass growing down into the well was slippery and hard to get ahold of. After a few minutes, I managed to work my way out of the well.

A few years later, there was more trouble. There was a farm near our house that wasn't used much anymore. My mom and dad farmed a little area on the land with a garden on the side. We also mowed down some bushes and made a Wiffle ball field, and that's where we played. But the blue-gray barn was still there.

One morning, a buddy of mine was over and asked me what was inside. I told him there was some cool equipment in there that I could show him, an old piece of farm equipment our neighbor had used to mow and bale grass and hay. It was all rusted out, just taking up space.

I was fascinated by the gears. I showed him how the machinery worked. Next thing you know my finger was smashed in between the two gears. I yanked out my hand and nearly pulled my left pinky finger off. The pain was excruciating, the worst pain I have ever felt. I held my finger and we sprinted up the hill to my house. My mother was a stay-at-home mom, and she was stunned initially, and then she immediately went into emergency mode. Our little town's population was about four thousand, so our medical facility was more of a doctor's office than a hospital. We had to go ten miles into Bellingham, where the big hospitals were.

I was freaking out, crying, hysterical. I thought I was going to lose my finger. They deadened it to dull the pain, and then they X-rayed it. They performed surgery to reattach the finger and repair the joint. There was a possibility I would have lost the finger from the knuckle up. That they were able to save it was a blessing for a quarterback. You need that finger to throw the football. I think of that incident every time I look at my finger.

I used to enjoy jumps on my bike. It's not like I was Evel Knievel and wanted to jump the Grand Canyon. But I did like the feeling of hitting a ramp to see how high I could go, how far I could jump. Some of the other kids didn't want to get hurt, but I really didn't think much about that. Let's just build a ramp, have a few kids over, and jump. I guess some of my tendencies from childhood have stuck with me through the years.

CHAPTER 3

UNDERDOG

My whole sports career I have been the underdog. Everybody has bet against me. I was always trying to prove myself. As a backup quarterback every year, I had to prove I belonged. As a coach, I learned that very few believed in me.

This has been the case for as long as I can remember. At Ferndale High School I played basketball, and we did not have a very good team. We weren't expected to win, but we loved the game. We figured out ways to beat some good opponents by playing team basketball. Our coach preached about making three passes before shooting, constantly moving the ball. So with our strategy, we sometimes figured out a way to win even though we weren't supposed to.

In football more was expected of our team, but we were underdogs in one game. The Ferndale Golden Eagles were the number-two-ranked team in the state, behind the Burlington-Edison Tigers, and we went on the road to play them. They were favored, but we embraced the challenge. We returned the opening kickoff for a touchdown, and then missed the extra point. That was all we needed. We ended up winning the game 6–0.

I was reminded of that game during the 2017 postseason. As I mentioned, nobody believed in us, even though we had earned home-field advantage in the NFC throughout the playoffs. The oddsmakers said we should lose every one of our postseason games. We felt disrespected. It made me mad, and I know it made the players mad too. I didn't verbalize it and show my anger, but it simmered beneath the surface. We played Atlanta as three-point underdogs at home. Then we hosted Minnesota and were three-and-a-half-point underdogs. Against New England, we were something like four-and-a-half- or five-point underdogs by kickoff.

Once we lost Carson, who was an MVP candidate, a lot of people thought we were just another team. But we were 13–3 in the regular season. We had the fourth-best defense in the National Football League statistically. We scored more points than every team except the Rams and Patriots. We had the third-ranked rushing offense. We had the eighth-best third-down conversion percentage. Everyone forgot we had the fourth-best takeaway/giveaway differential in the league.

So we embraced the underdog role. We used it as fuel and emotion. My approach was this—if it stirs something in us as players and coaches, let's use it. We trusted one another when no one else did. It was calculated to a degree. But it was real.

It really hit me when Lane Johnson and Chris Long wore dog masks after the Atlanta game. I didn't know what they were up to until I saw them walking around the field. I believe in allowing players to show their personalities, and here were Lane and Chris, showing the world that we embraced our role. We'd been treated like dogs and were underappreciated. That tied right into my messaging.

This attitude reflects our city. Philadelphia is a blue-collar town with tough, hard-working people. We play in South Philly where they have always prided themselves on earning everything they have. They take nothing for granted. So our fans' mentality inspired us. When we played the Vikings the next week, we saw a lot more dog masks in the stands.

The week of the NFC Championship Game, the NFL issued a poster promoting Super Bowl LII. It showed the Lombardi Trophy, which of course makes sense. But it featured the Patriots and the Vikings. And the conference championship games had not been played yet. The league took it down, but I still have a photo of the poster on my phone. That fueled everybody on our team. It was total disrespect to show the Vikings but not the Eagles. Our guys took offense. I took offense. But it only confirmed what we felt.

The truth is, even I had doubts heading into the Minnesota game. I was more nervous going into the NFC Championship than I was going into the Super Bowl because of the matchup with the Vikings. The whole week, I had let doubt creep in. It got into my head. I wasn't sure if we were going to be able to move the ball on the Vikings.

Let's not forget, the Vikings had the number-one defense in the National Football League. There were no weaknesses on tape. Still, I didn't think their offense was great. It was efficient, but they weren't scoring a ton of points. I was nervous for the players. But I felt if our defense could keep us in the game we had a chance.

I went out there with knots in my stomach. But when I watched our guys in pregame warmups, they were dancing around. They weren't acting like they were feeling any pressure. I looked over at the Minnesota side. They had a confident swagger about them. They had just beaten New Orleans, so that made sense. But there was a difference between us and them—our guys were looser. At that point, all my nervousness went away. It was the first time I had seen our team that relaxed, that juiced up, and that excited about a game the entire season.

Then on the opening drive, the Vikings went down the field and scored seven points. Doubt started creeping back. "Okay, it's going to be one of these games," I thought. We scored on their next possession when Patrick Robinson intercepted Case Keenum and brought it back for a touchdown, and then we took the lead on our next possession. The way we responded, I knew it was on. We scored thirty-eight unanswered points. It convinced me to never let doubt creep into my thinking again, to never doubt my players, and to always trust the process and preparation.

Jeannie had a better handle on it than I did. I came home one night the week before the NFC Championship and she asked, "How are the Vikings?" I told her they were really good. I said, "I don't know about this one." She said, "What do you mean? I used to watch you call plays at Calvary Baptist, and you destroyed people. This isn't any different." It brought me back and helped me focus. Jeannie tells me all the time that coaching in the NFL isn't much different from coaching in high school. The athletes are bigger and smarter. The opposing coaches are smarter. But it's not that complicated. If I continue to prepare and study situational ball and then study our guys and our opponents, it shouldn't be any different than it was years earlier, when I was head coach at Calvary Baptist Academy, a private high school in Louisiana. Jeannie always says I should be able to go out and carve up a team like I did back then. It isn't quite that easy, but to some extent she has a point. So I adopted that approach—I better believe in my ability to call plays and lead this team. She helped paint a picture for me, giving me more confidence.

Jeannie was there for me in 2016, when we were 7–9. We were mired in a five-game losing streak, which was difficult to take at the start of my head coaching career. I had doubts. Are we good enough? Am I what people said I was? "Where is your confidence?" she said. "It was fun watching you in high school. Your play calls were fantastic. I know you can call plays."

She was right. I took over Calvary in the second year of their football program. Our record was 41–10 in my four years there, with six of our losses coming in my first season. There were many times we weren't given a chance to win, but I had confidence in my staff and my team, and we had a lot of fun.

You talk about unique formations. I had goofy stuff all over the place. One play had ten boys at the line of scrimmage, stretched out sideline to sideline. The quarterback was alone in the backfield. He would yell, "Shift!" Certain guys would step back off the line before the snap so we were legal. One of two things would happen—a big play for touchdown because the defense didn't know what to do, or they'd burn a time-out. We would have pods of players on the left, on the right, and around the ball. We attempted fake field goals. It was truly thinking outside the box, and the kids had a blast.

They were a bunch of small players. Yet we were blowing teams out. My last year there, we traveled to Monroe, Louisiana, to play Richwood High School. Monroe became home to me when my family moved there in 1986, so this game was a pride thing for me. When the opposing team came out to warm up, we saw they were giants. I told our assistants, "We better hold on tight." This explained why we were fourteen-point underdogs. Richwood scored easily on the first drive, then we went three and out. Things improved from there. We forced a turnover and scored. We ended up winning 49–7. The preparation and hard work paid off. Our kids never wavered.

Fast forward eight years later, and very few people thought I would be selected as head coach of the Eagles.

I didn't even prepare to be interviewed prior to being contacted by the team because I didn't think I would be a candidate. A lot of people doubted that I would be the right person for the job. There were reports that Ben McAdoo was the Eagles' first choice. They also interviewed Adam Gase before me, and Tom Coughlin after me.

My history with the Eagles worked in my favor, I think. I played for them in 1999, and met Howie Roseman, who was on the scouting side and working his way up at the time, Jeffrey Lurie, and current team president Don Smolenski—a lot of the people who are still in the organization. When I came back in 2009 as an assistant for four years with Coach Andy Reid, they saw how I worked and interacted with others. By this time Howie was the general manager, and he and Andy had a great relationship. All that good history meant there were some good vibes.

By 2015, I had been with Andy in Kansas City for three seasons. We had a successful year and we were getting ready to play the Texans in the playoffs. That's when the Eagles sent a permission slip for an interview. I suspected it was coming. Andy was still close to the Eagles organization and spoke on my behalf to Howie and Jeffrey and the people who were making the decision. I give a lot of credit to Andy for helping me.

When they requested an interview, I scrambled to get

prepared. I was trying to game plan for that Saturday night's Texans matchup in Houston at the same time. The interview was scheduled for 8:00 the following morning in downtown Kansas City, where the Eagles contingent had flown in from Philly.

I had to be able to verbalize my coaching philosophy and talk to them about how my staff would look. With help from my agent, Bob LaMonte, I prepared a two-inch three-ring binder that explained everything. I had all the information organized and ready to go. A lot of it was in my head, too, and I knew it was important for me to speak from my heart as well. Meanwhile, we beat the Texans.

When I arrived at the hotel in Kansas City, Howie met me in the lobby and escorted me to one of the suites. It was very big, a presidential suite with a living room and a kitchen. I turned the corner and there was this beautiful dining room table, and everybody was sitting around it. I knew just about everyone in the room: Jeffrey Lurie, Don Smolenski, Howie Roseman, Senior Vice President Aileen Dagrosa, and a couple of others. I was like, "Hey, guys!" It was sort of calming to recognize the people I had worked with or played under when I had been a member of the Eagles.

Jeffrey's son Julian was there too. I helped train Julian when Julian was in high school and he wanted to be a quarterback. I was the quality-control coach at the time, and Jeffrey came to me and said, "Hey, would you mind teaching my son to throw a football and play the quarterback position?" I spent several sessions teaching and coaching Julian. Now here he was interviewing me.

I sat down and we exchanged pleasantries, talking about our families and that kind of thing. Then we got to business. Fortunately, everything came easily and flowed naturally. I felt I had good answers for their questions. There were some funny moments too. When the subject of training camp came up, I said, "I'm looking forward to going back to Lehigh for camp," not knowing they had moved camp from Lehigh University, in Bethlehem, Pennsylvania, to the NovaCare Complex in Philadelphia. And they said, "Well, you know we've moved camp." I said, "I got it," then told them I was all in for training camp at NovaCare. We had a good laugh.

I'll never forget the last thing they asked me to do. Howie said, "We're going to leave the room for ten minutes. When we come back, we will sit on the sofa over there and would like you to make a presentation. Act like we are your new team, your new players, and this is your first team meeting in the spring. Tell us what you would say to the team." So they exited the room, and I grabbed my notepad and jotted down my thoughts.

After they came back and sat down, I launched into my speech. I talked about how we would practice. I talked about the type of culture I wanted, how we would cultivate it. I talked about how we were going to play a certain way and act a certain way as Philadelphia Eagles. I said I didn't know what had happened in the past, but going forward, things would change. We would pay attention to little things. I talked about what I truly believed in. And finally, I shared the four things that would apply to anything and everything we would do.

"First, we need to create energy. Every day you players step into this building, you have to bring the juice. Every single day. I will too.

"Second, eliminate distractions. What are those? It could be dealing with people asking you for tickets to a particular game, or hotel rooms. It could be the media pulling at you. It could be your contract weighing you down. Whatever the distractions are, we need to eliminate them once we are in season.

"Third, attack everything. We will attack the way we train. We will attack the way we practice, the way we eat, the way we sleep, the way we study. That needs to be in your mind-set from day one.

"Fourth, fear nothing. Not our opponents, not failure, not anything in our lives."

When I finished with the presentation, that was the end of the interview. We said our goodbyes, and they returned to the airport. I went back to the office to prepare for our next game, against New England.

Later in the day, Howie called. He told me I did an outstanding job. He said they were comfortable with me, but he didn't offer me the job. He went over some of the interview, then thanked me for the time.

A few days later, I called Jeannie from the office and she said, "I just heard the news!" I'm like, "What news?" She said, "Ian Rapoport and Adam Schefter are saying you're going to be the next head coach of the Eagles. That's awesome!"

Officially, nobody told me anything, but I was excited anyway. Andy, after hearing the reports, came by to congratulate me. I hadn't heard from Howie or Jeffrey, though. We lost to New England that Saturday night. It was disappointing to lose in the divisional round of the playoffs after the season we had. When I was leaving Gillette Stadium some Philadelphia reporters were waiting for me, but I declined all interviews.

On the bus to the airport my phone rang. It was a 215 area code. I didn't recognize the number, but I picked up, and it was Jeffrey Lurie on the other end. He said he was sorry for the loss, but it was a great season. Then we talked about my interview, and he told me how impressed he was.

He said he wanted to officially extend the offer to me to become head coach of the Philadelphia Eagles. I was thinking, "Heck yeah! I'd love to accept the job."

We flew back to Kansas City, and I had one day to get my things together before flying to Philly with Jeannie. The day I officially signed was Monday, January 18, 2016, our twenty-fourth wedding anniversary. So it was kind of an anniversary gift.

They had a big press conference. Our auditorium holds maybe two hundred people, and it was standing room only. It was all a little overwhelming, but that night we relaxed over a nice dinner at Jeffrey's home with the same group of people who had come to interview me in Kansas City, along with their spouses and significant others.

The next day I hit the ground running. There were some coaches still in the building from Chip Kelly's staff who I wasn't going to retain, so I had to have some tough conversations with them. By nature, I'm not a confrontational guy, so that's one of the hardest things for me to do. You're really affecting somebody's life, and some of them were men who had been there for maybe only six months or so. But my philosophy was to bring in my guys and go to battle with them.

Speaking of which, I had to put together a staff. I had reached out to some assistants before I had the job, but I wasn't sure about the coordinator positions. I interviewed a handful of guys who were already on staff who I either knew or were recommended. I ended up retaining Jeff Stoutland as offensive line coach, Dave Fipp as special teams coordinator, Cory Undlin as secondary coach, Justin Peelle as tight ends coach, Matt Harper as assistant special teams coach, and Duce Staley as running backs coach. I have a lot of respect for these men.

I interviewed Jim Schwartz to be my defensive coordinator immediately. We sat down for about four hours and I felt really comfortable with him. He's a former head coach of the Lions, which was really beneficial for me. And he was a longtime defensive coordinator who used the Wide 9 technique, an attacking defensive front. Having coached against that scheme, I knew it presented problems for offenses. He would be a great resource for a first-time head coach too. I could ask him things, like "How did you handle training camp practices? How about your offseason? What did your meetings look like? How did you discipline players?"

For instance, the way I had the schedule the first season, we had practice directly after a forty-minute walk-through, with no break. So we were on the field for two hours and forty minutes straight. By the end of that year, the players felt worn out. After the season, Jim told me he thought giving the players time between the walk-through and practice would be beneficial. A break to get something in their stomachs, tape their ankles, soak in the hot tub, whatever they wanted to do. I took his advice, giving them a fifty-minute break in between. It was very helpful. He also had some useful suggestions for travel when we were crossing time zones.

I knew I would spend tons of time on the offensive side because that was my area of expertise, so hiring him freed me up. I could give Jim control and let him run the defense.

My next hire was Frank Reich, who was just let go by the Chargers, where he was the offensive coordinator for two seasons. I wanted him to be my offensive coordinator in part because he had been in charge of one of the top passing offenses in the league with Philip Rivers in San Diego. I wanted to blend our passing philosophies. We had played against one another when he was a quarterback in Buffalo and I was in Miami. His playing experience meant something because he could see the play through the eyes of the quarterback. We had known each other a long time. After he accepted, all the major pieces were in place.

It was mid-January and we needed to work on establishing an offensive identity, fixing a defense that ranked twenty-eighth in the league the year before, and improving things across the board. There were days I would sit there overwhelmed and wonder, "Am I qualified to do this? Am I really capable of doing this?" Who wouldn't want to be a head coach? But when you're finally in that chair and making decisions big and small, you're just like, "Man, I don't know."

I loved being a coordinator and being hands-on with the players and the offense as a whole. When you become the head coach, however, you get further and further away from teaching football. That was the hardest thing, knowing I wouldn't be as attached to the players. That's what I thought, at least, that this would be a lonely deal. Things began to pile up—meeting after meeting, examining the roster, free agency, and the draft. But I just couldn't step back and take a break. Every day, I pushed on and became a little more comfortable.

Meanwhile, critics were saying I was the worst head coaching hire of the year. I wanted to know why they said that. Was it because they saw me as an Andy Reid knockoff who wasn't my own man? Did they look at the track record in Kansas City or the success we had with Alex Smith? I had to block that out and trust myself. The outside world didn't matter. It was about the guys in the locker room. They are the ones I stand in front of every day. I had to get them to play for me, and to play for one another. That's what mattered. If I could get those guys to believe in me and follow me down this road, I knew we would be okay.

My first year we finished 7–9. I know I had a little bit of

the benefit of the doubt as a first-year head coach. It was the honeymoon phase. Most of the comments were okay, but coming off the field after games, there was always that one voice that was much louder than everyone else's: "Pederson, you suck! Go back to Kansas City! Wrong guy for the job!" When I heard that, sometimes I'd wonder all over again, "Am I really qualified to lead this football team?"

Every Monday I do a radio interview on sports-talk station WIP, on *Angelo Cataldi & the Morning Team*. Angelo was as nice as he could be, but I knew after we hung up he was going to rip me. That's how sports-talk radio in Philadelphia is. Even after we lost five in a row that first season, I was the most positive, upbeat guy come Monday. Angelo would ask, "Why are you always upbeat?" I would say, "The sun came up, we have a chance to get better this week, we have a great opponent coming up. We don't have time to be disappointed."

I keep a TV on in my office. Throughout the day, I bounce through different channels—NBC Sports, ESPN, or NFL Network. I want to listen to what our opponents are saying, and what people are saying about us. Sometimes, something is said that I can use as motivation for the team. As a rule, I try not to pay attention to the local media. Philadelphia is a tough, competitive market, and they can be hard on me and the team. Those reporters work hard, and I respect the job they do, but I stay away from the local media for the most part. I do like to have fun with the guys when they pick against us, though.

Before the 2017 season started, former NFL general manager Mike Lombardi was very critical of me. Lombardi, who now works for *The Ringer,* said, "He might be less qualified to coach a team than anyone I've ever seen in my thirty-plus years in the NFL." And he didn't stop there. "Everybody knows Pederson isn't a head coach," he said. "He might be less qualified to coach a team than anyone I've ever seen. When will the Eagles admit their mistake? Will they throw away 2017 by stubbornly sticking to the Pederson Principle?"

I don't want to say that it didn't bother me because somewhere deep down, I wondered why he would say that. What gave him the right, or what gave him the balls, to say that about a new head coach who had only had coordinating experience and was adapting and growing? I never even talked to the man. He had never done an interview with me. He never reached out and wanted to get to know me, but yet he went off and said I was the worst coach.

All of this came out the day before our season opener. One of our local writers picked up on it and went off chasing the rabbit. He connected Lombardi to Jim Schwartz because

Lombardi hired Jim on the Browns nearly twenty-five years earlier. So Jim was dragged into this, too, and it created a little tension between him and me. The writer was basically saying Jim was waiting for me to fail so he could become the next head coach of the Eagles. Jim saw the article and came down to my office. He was pissed—pissed at Lombardi, pissed at the writer. We were trying to prepare for the Redskins the next day, mind you. Jim said, "None of it is true, Coach. I haven't spoken to Michael about you. I haven't spoken to anybody."

We got through it, and won against Washington. The players had seen all the articles and heard the talk. So afterward, Kamu Grugier-Hill and Steven Means gave me the Gatorade shower. "Coach, that's for you," they said. "It's to let you know we're with you." That was cool and I appreciated it.

Fast forward to the week after the conference championship game. I had a collection of fan mail piling up at the office. One of them was a small envelope with an address but no name on the back. I opened it and pulled out a card. On the stationery it said, "Michael Lombardi." It was written on a typewriter, and was about three paragraphs long. The letter said, "The first rule of any informed opinion is to never begin with the end in mind. And I violated that rule. For that, I extend my sincere apology." I was appreciative, and at least it showed he was man enough to admit he was wrong. After the Super Bowl, the possibility of writing this book came up. One of the interested companies thought Lombardi would be a great coauthor and submitted an offer. I said, respectfully, "No thanks."

It wasn't the first time I had to deal with doubters and naysayers here in Philadelphia. When I was the quarterback of the Eagles in 1999, we used to come out of the tunnel at Veterans Stadium from the first-base dugout. Across the stadium on the second level, we usually saw a long banner that had something written on it that wasn't very nice. Some that stood out to me from that season: "PEDERSON, IT'S NOT PERSONAL." And right before the holidays: "ALL WE WANT FOR CHRISTMAS IS A QUARTERBACK." Finally: "HEY, MRS. REID & MRS. PEDERSON, YOU NEED TO GO SHOPPING FOR A NEW COACH AND A NEW QUARTERBACK."

There was verbal abuse too. While I was the starting quarterback, I was also the holder for extra points and field goals. During pregame warmups, one fan yelled, "Pederson, you need to go back to holding." Once, I was running off the field down the ramp. My family sat right up above the tunnel, so I was looking up and waving at them. Just then someone spit a big wad and nailed me right in the head. That pissed me off. Our team wasn't very good, so the coach and the quarterback were taking the brunt of the blame. You are either the hero or not, and at that point I was not.

But going through that experience only prepared me to come back into this environment and this city. I've been through it, and now I embrace the challenge. I learned how to block out the noise and overcome the doubt, and focus instead on the things that make me and the team better. That's what helps us win.

CHAPTER 4

A TEAM CAN MAKE A MIRACLE

Carson Wentz was limping back to the huddle, patting his leg right above his knee. I knew something was wrong. I thought it might be a thigh bruise, not a serious knee injury. He ran four more plays and finished up with a touchdown pass. He came to the sideline, and the doctors examined him in the medical tent. Our trainer came up to me and said, "We're going to take him to the locker room for more evaluations and X-rays." At that point, I knew without a shadow of doubt that this was not going to be good. After the game, I always meet with our doctors, and that's when they gave me the bad news—Carson had a torn ACL.

We beat the Rams in LA and won the NFC East in the process. But we lost Carson. It was bittersweet. We were 11–2 and Carson had thrown his thirty-third touchdown pass, which meant he was leading all quarterbacks in the National Football League. He was in the running for most valuable player. We were being talked about around the country as heavily favored to be in the Super Bowl. And now he was lost for the season and the playoffs.

The whole city of Philadelphia was crushed. The air went out of the room. There went our Super Bowl dreams, and there went our hopes. We would have to wait until next year. It was the "here we go again" Philadelphia mentality. This city has been let down time and time again by its sports teams, particularly by the Eagles.

The truth is, I was crushed too. I was sitting there thinking, "We had everything right there in front of us." But I would not allow myself to show how disappointed I was. I had to ask myself, "How do I, as the head coach, the leader, get the group through this one?" The good news was that I had a lot of experience in overcoming setbacks. I remembered all the things I talked about in my interview for the job—eliminating distractions, creating energy, attacking everything, and fearing nothing. On Monday at my press conference I used those principles.

When I walked into the team meeting on Tuesday, I could feel that the room was down. The team was defeated, as if a family member had just passed away. But I walked into that room with energy and juice. I basically told them, "Pull your heads out of your butts. We are still a good football team. We have one of the top defenses in the National Football League." I reminded the players, the coaches, the personnel staff, and other people in the organization standing in the back of the room what got us to that point. I reminded them that we lost Darren Sproles. We lost Jason Peters. Those guys are Pro Bowl players. We lost Chris Maragos, Jordan Hicks, and Caleb Sturgis. I had a special message. They had to understand something and remember it: "One man can make a difference, but a team can make a miracle." Howie had been down about losing Carson. But after that meeting, he waited for me to come out and he said, "You're absolutely right." His demeanor had changed, as had the demeanor of the rest of the team.

There's a great story on where that quote came from. I have a couple of photos in a frame on my basement wall. They were taken in 1998 when I was playing in Green Bay. In one photo are me; our quarterbacks coach, Darrell Bevell; Brett Favre; our strength coach, Barry Rubin; and country singer Tim McGraw. In the other photo are our wives with Faith Hill. The photos were taken backstage at the Tim McGraw concert in the Resch Center in Green Bay. I started listening to country music in college, and became a Tim McGraw and Faith Hill fan. I love his song "Live Like You Were Dying."

After Carson went down, my oldest son, Drew, was in the basement and he happened to be looking at the photo. He took a picture of it and zoomed in on something none of us had ever noticed before. On the wall over Brett's head was a sign with a quote—"One individual make can make a difference, but a team can make a miracle." It doesn't say who said it, and I have no idea why it's there, but there it is. Drew sent me the picture on Monday afternoon, explaining how he just came upon it.

I said, "Oh my gosh! That's it!" I thanked my son and I walked into the team meeting feeling a little better. I told the team the story about the photo, adding, "If you believe that one man can make a difference but a team can make a miracle, then our dreams and goals are still right in front of us." The quote became our theme the rest of the season.

Every Saturday night, I showed them a highlight video of the previous game if it was a victory. The video always ended with an eagle flying in, then transitioned to our logo. Our video guys brought me a new ending—the Lombardi Trophy with the quote, "One man can make a difference, but a team can make a miracle." I loved it, and we used it for every highlight video.

I kept reminding the guys that it never was about one guy. It wasn't about me. It wasn't about Carson. It wasn't about the other guys who were hurt. And it wasn't about any of the healthy guys. It was about all of us, together. That's what could make the miracle. The guys really embraced that. Because of that, you saw the resiliency of our team. Things could have easily unraveled after Carson went down. It could have gone the other way. Guys could have thrown in the towel and said, "This is hopeless. We're done."

I felt I needed to be an emotional leader at that time. If I was the one who was going to stand up in front of the team, I could not come in with my shoulders slumped, acting like "Woe is me." They would take one look at me and think, "Well, Coach feels that way. Must be bad. It must be over." It was a critical moment that brought the team together.

The importance of being a family, or a band of brothers, or whatever you want to call it, was reaffirmed. Of course, we had to deal with the challenges of having a different quarterback with different talents. Publicly, I was saying we didn't have to change much structurally in our offense. While we didn't need to overhaul the offense, we did need to find things within the offense that played to Nick Foles's strengths.

It took some time to figure out some of those things, watching tape and talking with Nick and putting all the pieces together. One of the things we did was eliminate some of the motion and shift plays. Nick was most comfortable just lining up and seeing the defense, without the presnap movement. So we lined up in the final formation without the moving parts. Once he became comfortable, we started bringing some of the motion back. The three games at the end of the regular season were like Nick's preseason, which he missed because of an elbow injury. And in the preseason, we usually eliminate the motions and shifts so the guys can play fast and just execute.

The other thing we did was use about 5 to 10 percent more run/pass option (RPO) plays. We called one probably at least every series. A lot of them were repeat plays but from a different personnel group. Nick came out of the Chip Kelly offense where it was all RPOs, so he was really comfortable with them. He thrived through the postseason with RPOs. It was a great way to get him settled into games, not to mention a great way to start drives because whether it was a run or a pass, we would usually gain eight yards.

Through the season, Nick always said that this was Carson's team. Even after Carson went down and Nick became the starter, he publicly said it. I thought Nick had to push that aside. I understood where he was coming from, but it was important for him to realize that at this moment, this was his team. After his first start, we had a really good conversation about it one night as he was wrapping up his day. We sat and talked for about forty-five minutes. Some of it was just small talk, some of it was about the offense, and some of it was about embracing his role as the leader of this team. "Why don't you go win a playoff game?" I said. "Why don't you go win the Super Bowl? You are a veteran guy. You've been there. You've done this." We talked about Carson being the future. We weren't taking that away from Carson. But at that moment, all eyes were on Nick Foles and we were designing our offense around him. I think that's when Nick really started to embrace the role. His mind-set became, "Yeah, this is my team and we'll go as far as I'll take them."

Losing a quarterback, especially one who was playing as well as Carson was, is different from losing a player at any other position. But as I told the team in that meeting room, Carson hardly was the first loss we had to overcome. All season long, we had to overcome one thing or another that was potentially devastating.

Coming out of training camp we were feeling very good about our special teams. Our kicker, Caleb Sturgis, was very accurate. On the opening kickoff against the Redskins in the first game of the season, he injured his groin, hamstring, and hip flexor of his kicking leg. He's a tough kid. He didn't say anything about it the entire game and he played through it. He kept kicking and even drilled a fifty-yard field goal as time expired in the second quarter. After he hit another field goal in the fourth quarter, I noticed him limping off the field. I asked if he was okay, and he said he was fine. My special teams coordinator, Dave Fipp, said he noticed it too. Then the medical people found out he was injured. On our last touchdown we went for two instead of having him kick again.

In the third week of the season, Darren Sproles went down with a fractured forearm and a torn ACL. He was our starting punt returner and our third-down back. He was a significant contributor, so a lot of production was gone from our offense. Chris Maragos went down with a torn ACL against the Panthers in our sixth game. He's a core, All-Pro special teamer and a backup safety. Then in the rematch against the Redskins in the seventh week of the season, we lost Jason Peters, our Pro Bowl left tackle and a team leader. We also lost Jordan Hicks, our starting middle linebacker. It was terrible watching these guys fall, but we didn't panic. We were prepared as much as we could be.

In 2017, I began a developmental program for all our young players. There isn't much player development going on around the league, and it's a problem. If we're not working with the bottom third of our roster, we're not maximizing our potential. I thought of ways to bring along our younger talent—the guys who normally don't play on offense or defense, or who might not play at all. On most teams, the guys who aren't playing hardly practice because the players who are playing need the reps to prepare. So the challenge is to develop those young players without taking away reps from the starters and their primary backups.

In the offseason, every other day during team periods—when it's eleven on eleven—I split the field. The starters were on field one. Everyone else was on field two. So now the nonstarters were getting the same number of reps that the starters were getting, with the same play calls. I carried it over to training camp. The only way you can get better at this game is to be on the field, so this helped a lot of players. During the season we spent ten minutes every Wednesday and ten minutes every Friday after practice taking the young players through individual periods with one-on-one work, teaching them the fundamentals and getting them back to some of the things we emphasized in camp.

This also helped develop our younger coaches, who normally don't get the chance to coach during the week—the quality-control guys and assistants to the assistants. Before the season, we gave them the job of coaching the young guys while the position coaches were working with the starters on the other field. During the season, they were getting to lead those drills after practice.

Eventually, a lot of those younger players were needed in games, and because we developed them along the way, they were ready to go. Among the players who benefited were Big V—Halapoulivaati Vaitai, Corey Clement, Rasul Douglas, Mack Hollins, and Shelton Gibson.

The next thing I knew, I had starters mixing in with the developmental players to get a few more reps in themselves. By the end of the season, I nearly had another full practice because almost everybody was on the field getting some kind of work in. And I truly believe it helped us.

I've heard some say that it doesn't make sense to develop your young talent. They will leave and go play somewhere else. That's kind of dumb and the wrong way to think. We had to prepare them for our team. It made our guys successful and helped us overcome many setbacks. This was a really good program that we'll continue.

Every team has setbacks in football. It's a big part of the game. If you can't deal with them, you have no chance. I experienced it as a player too. One of the worst times was in 1998, when I was with the Packers and we were playing the Vikings on *Monday Night Football*. It was Randy Moss's rookie season, and he and Daunte Culpepper just went off on us. Mike Holmgren was so mad. He started benching all the starters with about nine minutes left in the game. So I went in to replace Brett.

We scored a touchdown and closed the gap a little. Inside the two-minute warning we were in the red zone. Mike called a pass play. I dropped back, and the Vikings had a DB blitz on. As I let the ball go, Corey Fuller hit me with the crown of his helmet under my jaw. It felt like someone stabbed me, a piercing, intense pain. My pass was caught for a touchdown. That meant I had to hold for the extra point. I was bent over and holding my mouth, and there was blood trickling out. Ryan Longwell, our kicker, came over and asked me if I was okay. I literally couldn't even move my jaw to say anything. I just kind of nodded and mumbled. We lined up for the kick. I marked the spot and managed to say whatever I could to get the ball from the snapper, and Ryan made the kick.

Andy Reid, the quarterbacks coach at the time, told me we were going for an onside kick and I should be ready to go back in the game. I couldn't possibly play. The doctors were trying to stick their fingers in my mouth, and I was grabbing them and pushing them away. As it turned out, the onside kick failed. Thank you for that, I thought. They X-rayed my jaw after the game and saw it was broken. I spent the night at the hospital, where the pain just kept getting worse and worse. They performed surgery, and I woke up the next day with three wires in my jaw. It was wired shut for five weeks.

I couldn't put solid food in my mouth that whole time. There was enough of a gap for a straw, so I had mostly shakes. My favorite meal was Jeannie's chili, which I would puree in a blender. My mother-in-law used to work in a hospital, and she had these big syringes that let me suck up the chili and shoot it into my mouth. I lost about twelve pounds over the five weeks.

When they finally took the wires off, my jaw was so stiff and sore that I couldn't open my mouth, as if it were still wired. But I was craving a cheeseburger and fries. Jeannie took me to McDonald's, and when I put a French fry in my mouth and bit down, it brought tears to my eyes. The pain in my jaw and teeth and gums was excruciating from not using them. As I started moving my jaw a little more over the next couple of days, it got better. I eventually went back to practice, got myself back in shape, and resumed my role as the backup quarterback.

Brett had to overcome something more personal in 2003. I won't ever forget it. We were playing the Raiders on *Monday Night Football*, so we left on Saturday after a morning practice. On two-day trips, Brett and I always packed our golf clubs because we knew we would play somewhere the next day. On Sunday, we did our walk-through practice at Cal-Berkeley. After practice, we changed clothes and headed over the mountain to the Orinda Country Club, which was about thirty minutes from our hotel.

We played eighteen holes but still didn't have to be back for another couple of hours, so we decided to play part of the back nine again. Ryan Longwell and Josh Bidwell were with us, and as we were driving the carts, my flip cell phone rang. I opened it, and it was Brett's wife, Deanna. I could just tell something was wrong immediately by the tone of her voice. She asked if Brett was with me. Brett never carried his cell phone with him, so I passed it to him. His whole demeanor changed completely. He hung up and told us his father, Irv, was driving and had run off the road. He was being taken by an ambulance to a hospital. We left our balls on the green and took off. When we got back to the hotel, Brett found out his dad passed away on the way to the hospital. He had a heart attack while driving and then died in the ambulance.

We had our team meetings that night, but nobody was into football. Everybody was worried about Brett and his family. Here we were in Oakland, and everything for him was back in Mississippi. He was obviously distraught and beside himself. He was trying to process everything and didn't know if he would stay and play or head back to be with his family. Guys were in and out of his room, giving him support but also giving him his space. I was sitting there thinking, "All right, I'm going to have to play." Nobody said anything. I was kind of torn up about the whole thing.

Later on we had a team meeting. Our head coach Mike Sherman said Brett wanted to address the team. Then Brett came walking in, tears in his eyes. You could hear a pin drop. Guys were crying, sobbing. It was a pretty real moment. He told a couple of stories about his dad. He was trying to make a joke here and there and give us a little chuckle. That's Brett. Then he said he had been sitting in his room talking to his mother, his brothers, and his sister and trying to decide what to do. He said he kept hearing his father's voice. "Why the hell would you come back to Mississippi?" he was saying. "There's nothing to come back to. I'm gone. Stay and play ball with your teammates." Brett said Big Irv would not have wanted him to abandon his teammates. Then he said, "Tomorrow night, when we take the field, I've got your back." Everyone was like, "Whoa. He's got our back? We've got his back."

When we arrived at the stadium, I could tell his mind was far from the game. He put on his uniform and went through the motions and sat at his locker alone. It wasn't the Brett we were accustomed to. That Brett likes to have fun and keep everybody loose. There was none of that.

Then he went out and threw for 399 yards and four

touchdowns and we beat the Raiders 41–7. He had the most unbelievable game. To me, it wasn't only him. It was the guys around him. Some of the catches those guys made were on throws Brett never should have attempted. Guys were covered, and they were finding ways to get to the ball. Wesley Walls, Javon Walker—they were diving, jumping, catching touchdowns. They were making plays you just don't make.

The other cool thing about the game was how the fans responded. The fans in Oakland can be rough and tough with the Black Hole and all that. But the Raiders organization had a moment of silence before the game for Brett's dad. And then afterward, the fans gave him a standing ovation even though he just tore apart their team. It was so cool. It reminds you football is secondary to life. It's like when 9/11 happened, and you are reminded that football is not the most important thing.

Brett and I had a great relationship. Still do. We did a lot of things together. We golfed together and hunted together. Our families hung out. Our wives still are close. He knew that I was a Christian. And he found a little comfort in that, knowing there was somebody he could talk to. I don't think he could have a personal conversation with just anybody on the team. Brett's not like that. But because of our relationship, he trusted me. I let him know that I was praying for him and his family. We were able to talk about a lot of things other than football during that time and afterward. It was good to have him confide in me and share some personal things.

Looking back at it, I do think the experience helped him. I don't want to speak for Brett, but I think it shifted his priorities a little. He became more family oriented, more directed and focused. Other things became more important in his life than football and everything that goes along with it. You saw more humility in him. There was a quieter spirit. The more questions he asked, the more I could see him finding answers but still searching for more.

There are setbacks in the game and in life, and it's how you respond that matters. You talk about overcoming a setback—Brett was a great example of refusing to be kept down.

CHAPTER 5

WHY BE NORMAL?

'm the type of person who thinks for himself. I don't follow the crowd. As a play caller, I try to do things differently from other coaches. If you do what everybody else does, it's "Here comes this play again." Why not run the ball on third down when everybody is expecting you to throw it? That was part of our success in 2017. We were able to get to some fourth and ones and stay on the field with creative play calls on third down. Thinking out of the box, coming up with creative ways to use our personnel, and then knowing when to call plays can work to your advantage.

I'm a big believer in keeping it fresh, keeping it exciting, and keeping it fun so it doesn't get stale for the players. Stay aggressive. Why be normal? Sometimes people don't understand that. They question why I do some of the things I do in the course of a game. They say, "You can't do that in football; you aren't allowed." As I've said, I do it because I trust my players, I trust my coaches, and I'm not like everybody else. I'm going to do things my way, not the way others think it should be done or have been done. I want to have a gadget or a trick play in the game plan every week. Whether I call it or not, I want to have it available. Knowing when to call it is the key to a lot of the success. You have to have a method to the madness.

I learned a lot about being creative with structuring offense, play design, and play calling from Andy Reid. If you dive into what he does, you will see how creative he is. He sometimes thinks way out of the box. When I worked for him, we had to bring him a little closer to the box at times. When I looked at some of the routes he designed, I would say, "Coach, there is no way we can run these—it's information overload in the game plan." It was my job to come up with the name, the protection, and the formation for them. We ended up calling one Teepee because it looked like a teepee when we drew it up. That creative mind of his always was flowing.

A lot of coaches don't listen to their players, but I do. I

know it goes against conventional wisdom. After all, coaches are the ones studying the tape all day, right? But we're not the ones playing the game—they are. So if my offensive lineman says, "Hey, Coach, we can really run this play," I'll listen to him. It's a two-way communication, and I value what they see on the field. That's part of my process. I've talked about it publicly and had good responses on that from coaches around the league. I listen to my players in how we practice too. It's almost a reward. If they keep showing consistent improvement, then I'll listen to them. If I see or hear at any time that they are sluggish or tired, practices are starting to dip off, that's a sign to back down, to pull the pads off, to do something different to keep them fresh on game day.

We did a lot of walk-throughs toward the end of the season this past year. Then a few guys—Malcolm Jenkins, Fletcher Cox, and Jason Kelce—came to me and expressed an interest in putting the pads back on. They felt they were missing a little of the physicality, a little of the timing in execution. So I told them to put them back on, and it paid off. They were able to execute and fly around and do some good things in the playoffs.

We scored about ten touchdowns in 2017 on a red-zone concept that was suggested by Carson. He brought it to us from his playbook at North Dakota State. They called the play Mario, so we kept the name the same. The first time we used it was the third week of the season against the Giants. We had the play designed for Zach Ertz. He was wide open on the play on second down inside the five, but Carson shot the ball a little high and it whistled right through his hands. So I called the exact same play, but I put Zach in motion across the formation instead. We banged them for a touchdown. The play was a keeper.

I'm a traditional West Coast offense disciple. When I looked at Mario, I saw it as a twist on a West Coast concept. It was similar to a play Bill Walsh ran in San Francisco, and then Mike Holmgren took it to Green Bay. Now it's one of my favorite plays, and we try to find ways to get different guys in the position, different formations for the play, and different route combinations every week. It all came from Carson.

When a player comes to me with something, I don't automatically accept it. I want to know the whys. Why does he like the play? What defense does he like it against? What situations? Where on the field will it work? I do the same thing with the staff. I know why I like a play, but why do you like it? Show me some clips, some cutups of this play. Convince me to put this play in the game plan.

I know what it's like as a player to go to a coach and express an idea, and either have it accepted or rejected. When I was a backup in Green Bay, there were a couple of times when I suggested a play. One was called Double Arrow Eagle Cross. When I explained it to Darrell Bevel, our quarterbacks coach, I talked about how it was good against any defense. It had answers for everything. I wanted to add it to a game plan, and ultimately it was, against the Giants in 2004. Unfortunately, the play was never called.

It was Alex Smith who introduced me to run/pass options in 2013 when we brought him to Kansas City. He had used a lot of them when he was in San Francisco with Jim Harbaugh and Colin Kaepernick. Using RPOs helped us in Kansas City and in Philadelphia. With the Eagles, I have Jeff Stoutland, Justin Peelle, and Duce Staley, coaches who were here with Chip Kelly, who brought RPOs into the NFL from Oregon. So we've been able to grow our RPO package to the point where it's pretty dynamic and diverse. With RPOs, the quarterback decides what to do based on his read of a specific defender. Now we are constructing plays so the quarterback isn't always reading the same guy.

I've heard players from other teams criticize our offense. After we played the Vikings, one of the Vikings players called us a high school offense. Same thing with the Denver Broncos. We hung fifty-one points on them, and after the game we heard comments like "We had a hard time knowing where the ball was going to go from that high school offense." I don't know what he was trying to say, or if he was trying to pay us a compliment. Call it a high school offense, call it gimmicky—whatever you want. But if it helps us win games, I'm all about that.

Even Jon Gruden said our offense was gimmicky and not really an NFL offense. But you have to understand that all the kids who are right out of college, that's what they're used to. One-word plays, code words, playing fast, playing tempo. Again, it goes back to why do we have to play conventional football? I mean, yes, we have to line up legally, seven on the line of scrimmage, eleven on the field. They have to be in line with the rules. But after that, who says we have to be conventional? Why can't I think freely in my job, within reason?

We're taking advantage of having smart quarterbacks too. That's the trigger with RPOs. A smart quarterback makes you right on every play. And then it helps to have receivers who can run the routes that give them opportunities to catch more balls. RPOs look a little like play-action passes. Why are you going to run against a seven-man box when you can easily throw it to the perimeter, or you can ask your quarterback to carry it? I don't like to have the quarterback run a lot. I'd rather give it to a back or throw to a receiver. But it's the quarterback's decision. We're always working on finding new route combinations, or new ways of reading it.

Conventional wisdom says we're going to run the ball all the time and not give the quarterback a chance to throw it. People ask, "How are you going to protect the quarterback if you are reading a defensive end? You're not going to block him and ask the quarterback to throw the football? That's not conventional." But you can read the defensive end. If he's up the field trying to get to the quarterback, we're going to run the ball. If he takes two steps forward and then moves to play the run, the quarterback is going to keep it, not hand it off. So the defensive end can't be right. It makes sense.

This is what Alex brought us in Kansas City. We slowly evolved into a run game that gave the quarterback the ability to not have to always check a play, to audible at the line of scrimmage. It allows you flexibility as a play caller.

A lot of coaches have gone away from physical training camps. Not me. When I first took the job as Eagles head coach, I made a big point of putting the pads on in camp and hitting. We are probably in the upper 5 percent of teams in terms of physical camps.

We play a contact sport. Everything we do is hitting. Why wouldn't you hit in training camp to prepare your body, to prepare your head and neck for the physical nature of the game? If the first time you hit somebody is in the first preseason game, that's not right. You need to hit before that game. If you aren't conditioning the torso, shoulders, and neck to hit through contact in practice, your team will lose players.

I'm not saying you have to hit every single day. I have three live practices—tackle-to-the-ground practices—every training camp. Quarterbacks are never touched. At first, some of the administrative people thought that was crazy. In today's football, doing it this way is a little unconventional, but I've seen it work.

Andy liked to hit and we hit in Kansas City, too, but we're hitting more in Philadelphia. There are probably five practices during camp when I do take the pads off. So we might go four days in a row in pads, and the fifth day will be shells, shorts, and helmets. I also let them sleep in a little longer on those days, and the practices are shorter and crisper.

Over the course of the year, I get a lot of questions from the media about my use of analytics. Some teams use analytics more than others. That's okay. I understand why some coaches are skeptical. We are used to dealing with players, with human beings, and sometimes using numbers makes you lose the human element. Analytics can tell you some of the truth, but they don't tell you everything. You still must have conversations with your coaches and players, watch the film, and dive in further than simply reading data. So for me, it is about finding the right balance.

I want to find what is real when it comes to football. Numbers at the end of the day don't play games—people play games; players play games. I still have to motivate the team, I still have to lead the team, I still have to prepare the guys to play. We still have to teach fundamentals and do all the things that lay the groundwork for Sundays. The numbers may say we're better than this team and we should win, but it doesn't work like that. On the other hand, when it comes to situational football—two-point plays, third downs, fourth downs, red zone—and the numbers say I have a better chance to win the game by following a trend, I'm going to do it.

When I was in Philadelphia and Kansas City as an assistant for Andy, we didn't use analytics much. But part of the process of becoming a head coach in Philly involved talking about analytics and sports science and things that could potentially make a difference. I was honest with them and admitted I didn't have a lot of exposure to it. When I began studying the reports from our analytics people in Philly, it was overwhelming.

Jeffrey Lurie is also a big proponent of analytics. We

have weekly meetings and we often discuss reports and studies that our analytics team puts together. In a typical game week, I look at these reports for at least an hour every day with Ryan Paganetti—whether it's on our opponent's defense or a league-wide trend that helps us prepare. I spend more time on Mondays and Tuesdays than the rest of the week. On our opponent's numbers, some of my staples are percentage of coverages within offensive personnel groups, and coverages based on formation.

In the offseason, I'll also spend time on analytics. Some of the sports science information is over my head, and I don't want to get caught up in things that take me away from the game. But if it's something that can give us an edge, then I'm going to look at it. In the offseason we did a thorough evaluation of our offense, cutting up the season and breaking down the numbers. We spent about two hours every morning on tape and another hour crunching numbers. Sometimes you are pleasantly surprised in a certain area, and sometimes you are greatly disappointed because you know you could have been a lot better. There is one area of our offense that we thought we were pretty good at. Then we looked at the numbers, and it wasn't up to our standard.

With respect to situational ball, it helps me make clearer decisions and be more aggressive. And that does correlate to winning at times. Of course, there are other factors too. How are the players executing? How well are we playing offense? Defense? Then I can look at the numbers. If it's fourth and two at the opponent's thirty-eight, what do the numbers say here, and how does it mesh with the circumstances?

When we were evaluating quarterbacks for the draft, there were a lot of studies looking at Carson, Jared Goff, Paxton Lynch, and the others. You can go height, weight, speed, and hand size, and also dive more into how they think. There are tests out there that analyze reaction times, how fast they can process information. That is important at that position. Carson tested off the charts, making our decision that much easier.

The more I'm exposed to analytics, the more I can appreciate their value. And I'll get more out of them as I gain more experience in their usefulness.

I've been doing things differently from other people for a long time. There aren't many former NFL players who want to coach at a high school level, but I found it rewarding. And it really isn't that much different from coaching at the NFL level. You experience some of the same joy and excitement. It's on a bigger stage in the pros, but football is football. It's still blocking and tackling and trying to move our pieces better than they move their pieces. It's all about teaching your players and making sure they are ready to go on game day.

I'm really glad I did it, and will always be grateful to Calvary Baptist Academy for the opportunity. Maybe after I retire from the NFL, I could go back to coaching high school for a couple of years. But I just didn't see myself doing it the rest of my life.

Another thing that I approached differently was contract negotiation. Late in my playing career, I went against the grain and represented myself. For most of my career I used Benji Geller as an agent, and he did a nice job for me. But the rules had changed and there were minimum salaries. As a veteran, I knew I had to be paid at least $765,000 due to the collective bargaining agreement between the NFL and the NFLPA. I had a thought—why am I paying 3 percent of my salary on money the agent doesn't even negotiate? I spoke to Benji about it and suggested I would pay him 3 percent of anything above $765,000. He didn't like that, so we agreed to part ways.

So my last two years of playing for the Packers, I walked into Andrew Brandt's office. He was their vice president of player finance and negotiated all their contracts. We had some small talk. "How was your summer? Family doing good?" Then it was, "Here you go." I signed the contract for the league minimum and walked out. In 2004, my last year, the Packers also didn't force me to accept a split clause. With a split clause, they only pay you for a portion of the contract if you are hurt. As it turned out, I broke my back and went on injured reserve. It allowed me to receive my full salary. Not doing what everyone else is doing usually works out pretty well for me.

CHAPTER 6

CHEMISTRY

Chemistry is everything to any team, whether it's sports or business. Without good chemistry, the Eagles would not have accomplished what we did in 2017. If you have great chemistry and people work together well, you can overcome a lot of obstacles. You can win a lot more games with good chemistry than without it.

It starts with having the right people in the right spots. For us, it started with Carson Wentz. He is the face of the franchise and the leader of our team. In 2017, his second season, he became a lot more vocal. That was important. Our chemistry improved over time as we empowered the veteran players, guys like Fletcher Cox, Malcolm Jenkins, Brandon Graham, Jason Peters, and Darren Sproles. I encouraged them to say things in team settings and to give a closing thought to the team at the end of practice.

When we started offseason work, we had added new guys, and then after the draft we added a bunch of rookies. So that changed things. We had to meld all of the personalities into the group. Once everyone was on the same page, it formed the glue that kept everything together. The players enjoyed coming to work and being with one another. The chemistry built through the offseason and became stronger in camp. By the time we got to the regular season, we had a group that was strong enough to handle just about anything that was thrown our way.

Carson invited his receivers to Fargo, North Dakota, where he went to school, to work out and have a little fun. They went skeet shooting and horseback riding, and he showed them another part of the country. They also got some football work in. They all went—Alshon Jeffery, Torrey Smith, and Nelson Agholor. Some of the rookies couldn't afford the trip, so Carson paid their way.

People see how Carson plays on game day. What they don't see is how he interacts with teammates, coaches, and support staff in the building. He's in constant contact with his teammates and always is working at strengthening relationships. He does things you've seen Peyton Manning, Tom Brady, Drew Brees, and Aaron Rodgers do. With guys like that, it's not about them. And it's not about Carson Wentz. He's about wanting winning and success. He's a natural leader, with the ability to raise the talent level around him. I saw something similar in Dan Marino and Brett Favre when I was their teammate. They have a special gift that not many people have, and it's one of the reasons we chose Carson in the draft.

I also saw that special quality in another draft prospect in 2012 when I went to Madison, Wisconsin, to work out Russell Wilson. I was the Eagles' quarterbacks coach at the time and spent a whole day with him. There was an on-the-field workout, classroom time, and lunch together. I also met some of his friends. Seeing him interact with his teammates and friends, and seeing the respect everyone had for him, meant something. Of course, the football side of it was impressive. He was off the charts with his football IQ and athleticism. But there was something more. He had the "it" factor: he was a special player. I knew wherever he ended up, he would be successful. All you had to do was look at his history. He was successful at North Carolina State playing baseball and football. He transferred to Wisconsin and was voted a team captain within weeks of hitting the ground. Then he led them to the Rose Bowl.

I did not have an issue with him being five feet ten. He played behind the third-largest offensive line in college football that year and only seven of his passes were tipped at the line. It's all about how you use a quarterback—with a shorter guy you use play action. With Wilson, get him on the move where he can be accurate and his baseball skills take over. He can throw on the run like a shortstop or a second baseman. His movements are so fluid. We loved Russell. We were going to draft him, but Seattle got to him first. He went in the third round. We also really liked Nick Foles, so we chose him fourteen picks later.

When I visited Carson at North Dakota State before the draft two years ago, I was reminded of visiting Russell at Wisconsin. We pulled up, and Carson was waiting for us. He greeted us, held the door to the facility, escorted us in, and showed us where to go. As we spent some time in the classroom, I had flashbacks of Russell. I thought, "This kid is special." Of all the guys we worked out that spring, he had the right mentality, the mental toughness, the physical toughness, the love of the game. He had a lot of the same characteristics as Brett, though Brett could be a little more reckless and Carson was more controlled. Still, you got the same type of vibes from them. He is a proven winner who has been successful his whole life. He'll tell you story after story about competition. You know the tabletop game of paper football? He wanted to beat everybody at that game. Or if he was playing Nerf basketball, he had to win. On top of that he was a tremendous athlete and good passer. He checked all of the boxes for me. "He's going to win a lot of games," I told the front office. And Frank Reich, John DeFilippo, Howie Roseman, and Jeffrey Lurie agreed.

It was the intangibles that separated Carson from the other quarterbacks in that draft. You can look at the height, weight, and speed, the measurables, and they all are pretty similar. Intangibles, though, are critical. I spoke to coaches and former teammates. How is he in the locker room? How is he in the huddle? Does he have a commanding presence? Is there confidence when he speaks? Do guys listen? You have to ask these questions.

I also put a lot of emphasis on decision-making, timing, and accuracy. Touchdown-to-interception ratio tells you about decision-making. You can see timing on film. How well does he anticipate windows? Can he shape a throw around a defender? When judging accuracy, you look at the film to see if his passes are catchable balls. Are his throws one foot in front of the numbers, or are they always on the back hip, the back shoulder, or out in front where the receiver has to stretch to get it?

I also look hard at what we call unscheduled plays, which are improvisations. How well can he drop down, slide left and throw right, or slide right and throw left with accuracy? He also has to have a physical presence. The quarterback needs to be able to stand in the pocket and take a hit and still deliver a strike fifteen yards down the field. Carson did that. Russell Wilson did that. And Nick did it coming out of Arizona. He could take a beating and still deliver the ball.

I met Nick prior to the 2012 draft. I was supposed to visit Brock Osweiler at Arizona State and work him out, but I canceled for Nick, flying to Austin, Texas. I stayed near the University of Texas campus and ate at Eddie V's Prime Seafood around the corner from my hotel. The next day I met Nick at Westlake High School, where he had been a star. I told him where I had dinner. "Oh really, how did you like it?" he asked. I said it was a classic steakhouse and I had a great steak, enjoyed the atmosphere. He said, "Good, because my dad is an owner of that restaurant!" That led to us talking about his father and how he got into the business. Turns out he was involved in managing some of the Shoney's restaurants years ago. That was our first connection, talking about his dad and how he grew up. It was a great conversation and I could see he was a humble kid.

Once we got on the field for the workout, Nick's personality began to show. He was more relaxed, and a little more vocal. We talked about routes and combinations. I explained some of the routes that I wanted him to throw

as we discussed defensive coverages. I watched how he processed coverages as a quarterback coming out of college and
was really impressed with that.

He had a really good on-the-field workout. After a couple
of hours, we finished with some deep throws. The first one
was poor, coming out of his hand and wobbling like a lame
duck. So he asked if he could do it again, and threw a freaking rope. Then I thought, "This kid has a really nice arm."
We went into the school and I noticed all of these basketball
pictures on the wall. Nick pointed to one of him with his
teammates. He was a really good player and probably could
have played in college, but he chose football. We talked
about that a little bit, how the footwork of a basketball player
and a quarterback correlate.

They set us up in a little room and we went through some
college tape of his for another two or three hours. One of the
things I like to do is question draft prospects on their recall
of their offense. Can you give me the formation? Can you
give me the motion or shift, if there is any? Can you give me
the play? Describe the play to me. What is it best against?
What is this pass route right here? Tell me the strengths
and weaknesses of the protection and take me through all
of that. I was blown away by just how much he really understood football.

Nick wasn't as highly regarded as some of the other

quarterbacks in the draft that year, like Russell. In fact, I was the only coach from an NFL team who worked him out before the draft. He didn't have a great senior season at Arizona, but there were reasons for it. He had true freshmen on the offensive line blocking for him that year. They had so many injuries at wide receiver they had to play a converted defensive back. So his passing numbers and his completion percentage were down and his sack numbers were up. When you looked at those numbers, you said, "Eh, just an average guy."

But when I saw the tape of Arizona against USC from his senior year, that showed me all I needed to know about how competitive he was. Without his normal complement of linemen and receivers, he took shot after shot after shot and stood tough in the pocket. He got crushed by USC's pass rush. It was a shootout-type game, and he stood in there throwing strikes all over the field while being hit repeatedly. He just kept getting up and jumping back in there. I saw that same never-say-die attitude again in the Super Bowl. He was hit a couple times by the Patriots, hard, yet kept delivering.

I learned a lot about him that day in Austin. Having played the position myself, I had a good feeling that he would be a very successful NFL quarterback. I did think he was similar to Russell. He's a little more soft-spoken, more reserved, and laid back. It might take him a little time to adapt, maybe a little longer than Russell because he wasn't asked to do as much in his offense in college. Russell could change protections and all that, which Nick was comfortable doing but not as much, so there would be a learning curve. But he's a smart guy and he prepares. He blew the doors off for me.

Nick didn't play a lot in his rookie year when I was his position coach, but he told me how much he appreciated all of the football he learned that year, more than in any other. The next year, after I left for Kansas City, he made the Pro Bowl playing for Chip. Nick considered retiring after the 2015 season for a number of reasons, but he decided to play for the Chiefs. And in 2017, he was interested in working with me again. He always appreciated my predraft visit. Sometimes you might think something like that wouldn't be a big deal. But to Nick, it was. So we were probably the only team he felt comfortable going to, and signing him was a no-brainer. He was one of the guys I stood on the table for. I knew his work ethic, that he would spend the necessary time with me, and what he was capable of.

We also needed a veteran backup to Carson. And Nick was the perfect guy for our team chemistry. He'd be a great teacher and mentor to Carson, and he would support him in a way that Carson wouldn't get the feeling that Nick was trying to take his job. That's the mind-set of a great backup quarterback. I saw great leadership in him—an unselfish, disciplined player who is coachable.

No players impact your chemistry like a quarterback, but we had other acquisitions who helped in that regard. Chris Long was a veteran defensive end who had come off a Super Bowl with the Patriots, and we signed him as a free agent. He fit in our defense well, not to mention our locker room. His leadership brought a calming presence to the defensive line, the defense overall, and the entire team.

We don't just pull guys from around the league to sign. We have a blueprint—this is what an Eagles player should be like; these are the character traits they should have. The most important factor to me is that they love football, that they are ballers. They might not be the most talented guys, but if they have some of the intangibles, they will be coachable. And if they want to learn, you will win more games with them than with superstars who think they are too good to be coached. A guy like Chris Long wants to be coached, still has an edge, and still can produce and lead vocally on the field. Having him was a huge asset to our team.

Even with high-character players, the head coach still has to provide structure in order to have the best possible chemistry. That means having rules and enforcing them. They could be minor. For instance, for practice, they must wear the proper shoes, and they are not allowed to wear tinted eyeshields unless it is recommended by a doctor. It affects their vision, and I don't want that. Undershirts have to be tucked into their practice pants or shorts. In the cafeteria, they have to wear shirts with sleeves. No cutoffs or tank tops. They should look professional, and we don't need any body hair falling into the salad bowl. They can't have bare feet in the cafeteria, but they are allowed to wear sandals or tennis shoes. I don't want somebody slipping and falling or cutting their foot. It's common-sense stuff.

We start our meetings during the season at 8:15 in the morning, so all the players have to be in the building by 8:00. No cell phones are allowed in the meetings unless a wife or girlfriend is expecting a child or someone is ill. These are little things, but they can turn into big things. There is a certain level of discipline in our jobs we have to maintain.

It carries over to their football assignments. If they don't do the little things right, they won't do the big things right. On the field, those "little things" are details like eye placement, hand placement, all the nuanced body movements— lateral steps, vertical steps, drop steps. Being off just a bit can be the difference in a play being successful or unsuccessful.

If players don't comply with the rules, they get fined. If they are late in the building in the morning or have the wrong shoes, they can be fined a maximum of $2,490. I usually don't hit them with the maximum fine if it's a first offense. Maybe I'll fine them $750 the first time to get their attention. If it keeps happening, I'll keep increasing the fine. If a guy doesn't get to the building until after 9:00 a.m., it can be expensive. He can be fined for missing the 8:00 a.m. reporting deadline, then fined again for being late for the 8:15 special teams meeting, and then fined again for missing the 9:00 team meeting. Those three fines can add up to significant money.

I hold them more accountable for missing treatments because a player would be acting to the detriment of the team by not taking care of his injuries. Not showing up for a treatment will result in two fines—being late for the treatment as well as missing the treatment.

If they lose an iPad, they can be fined $13,285, plus the cost of a new iPad. I have never fined anyone that much, though. I usually fine them the cost of a new iPad, plus maybe $1,000. The fines hold them accountable and keep them focused. Early in the year, there usually are a lot of fines. By the end of the season, there are hardly any. I did have a couple guys late for meetings the week of the NFC Championship Game and I fined them. I know when a guy is trying to pull the wool over my eyes, but these were good guys who were simply late. There were no fines Super Bowl week.

I also believe in treating my players like adults. During our bye week, I give the players the whole week off. I tell them, "I know you guys are going to be traveling—on vacation or going to your homes. So you had better check the weather when you come back to Philadelphia so you are in the building Monday morning at 8:00 a.m. I'm going to treat you like men and treat you with respect. But if you abuse the privilege, I can keep you here and we can practice during the bye week." When I give them the leeway, they are respectful of the rules. We haven't had any issues.

Some coaches believe in giving star players preferential treatment. That isn't the way I do it. You have to remember I was a backup. I treat everybody the same. If a starter is late for a meeting, I fine him just like I fine a backup. There are no exceptions. I hold everybody accountable. I want them to hold me accountable too. After all, our jobs depend on the men next to us doing their part.

I find that everybody wants some form of discipline. Everyone wants to be held to a standard. This is why I put so much back on the team. If there is one bad apple, it's easy to remove the apple. It's another thing for the team to surround him, build him up, embrace him, and show him the way. This is the way we do things around here. Everyone needs to buy into what we are doing.

Players don't view me as a hard-core disciplinarian. I'm a big believer in being accessible and visible to the players. I try to visit the locker room two or three times every week.

It's usually in the morning before we head out for a walk-through. It gets me out of my office and lets me spend some time with the players, even it's only five or ten minutes. The point is to let them see me there and have a little give and take. It's a good way to find out if somebody has any issues. If a guy is down and out and I see him sitting at his locker, I have a chance to sit there and talk to him about it. It's getting to know guys and building relationships. I might ask one of the veteran players what he thinks about my practice plan for the day. "I'm going to cut back reps in practice. Are you okay if I cut it in this area?"

After fourteen years as a player in the league, I know the dynamic of a locker room and I'm very comfortable there. The locker room is the players' sanctuary. It's where they go to escape reality, meetings, and work. So it's a good place to interact. Some days I'm down there playing with them on the Pop-a-Shot basketball game. Letting my hair down occasionally and being one of the guys for a short period of time lets them see I am real and I have their best interests at heart. If I'm sitting in my office with my door shut I can't expect that to happen. I think it really helped our team build chemistry, as well as their trust in me and their trust in the process.

Another little touch is music. The players like to have it at practice, so we have allowed it. We started playing music during my last two years in Kansas City, and I brought it to Philadelphia. We play the music during team stretch and the competitive periods of practice as well as during special teams. Players—like people everywhere—are constantly having their minds stimulated, especially by their mobile devices, whether it's social media, videos, or music. So they are used to the noise. Music at practice keeps the guys light and helps them focus on their jobs. When I was playing, people thought music would be distracting to players. That's no longer the case. The songs are selected by players on the leadership council, as well as by Spencer Phillips, my assistant in 2017. But I have final say on it. The lyrics must be clean. I don't want any foul language, especially during training camp when we have fans out there.

Happy players are part of chemistry. With the Eagles in 2017, I saw it week in and week out. It got stronger every game. You could see how they loved to come to work every day. I can't say it's that way everywhere. I want to create an environment where they learn and grow and get better as individuals and as a team. As you can tell by my locker room visits, I pay attention to the feelings of my players. When guys are smiling as they walk out to practice, that's a good thing. When they walk out with their shoulders slumped and are hating life because they know practice is going to be a grind, that's obviously not so much of a good thing. If they are having fun at practice, you know games are going to be more fun. We didn't have a lot of guys try to get out of practice. They wanted to get better, not spend two hours in the training room separate from their teammates.

The only team I've been on that was similar in terms of chemistry was the Green Bay team that won the Super Bowl in 1997. We had great veteran leadership with Reggie White, LeRoy Butler, Brett Favre, Mark Chmura, and Eugene Robinson. It was very similar to the Eagles Super Bowl champions with Fletcher Cox, Malcolm Jenkins, Carson Wentz, Jason Peters, and Darren Sproles. Even after some of those guys were hurt, they still had a leadership presence. And my messaging to the team about staying consistent and believing in themselves was a lot like what Mike Holmgren did back in the day for the Packers.

Chemistry doesn't just happen. You have to plan for it and work on it. The Packers did it back then. We did it in 2017.

CHAPTER 7

FAITH AND FAMILY

As you can imagine, being the head coach of a team in the National Football League can be very stressful. There is a lot of outside pressure and scrutiny on a head coach, especially in a town like Philadelphia. In addition to what others say and think, we coaches tend to put a lot of pressure on ourselves and hold ourselves to a very high standard. Managing stress is important because you can't do your best if you're too stressed out.

As coaches go, I'm pretty laid back. But there is probably a reason for that: I'm a Christian and I have faith. I learned a long time ago not to worry about things I can't control. Life is too short. My hair started going gray in high school, so I already have enough gray hair. I'm only going to focus on today. I'm not going to worry about tomorrow or Sunday or next week. We have Dr. Kevin Elko speak to our team from time to time. He is a leadership coach who has some great inspirational messages. He likes to say, "Be where your feet are." That's so important. By being here now, I will maximize this time here.

It really helps me to start each day with some quiet time, reflecting on life, my challenges, and whatever God wants me to hear that day. I'm in my office about 5:30 every morning and sit at my desk and spend thirty minutes alone in my chair with no distractions. I take a couple of deep breaths and put my day in perspective. I grab my prayer book, *Jesus Calling*. There is a devotional and a scripture on each page. It takes two minutes to read, but the messages are powerful. Then I start journaling. I dive into my Bible a little. I say prayers—whether it be for the team, my family, or a friend or loved one who is struggling with something. I bring all of that to God in the morning. As I'm driving to work, I often wonder how I will accomplish everything that I need to get done that day. This quiet time sets the tone for my day and focuses me, puts me at peace. At the end of the day, I always look up and realize that everything is done that needed to be done.

If I don't start like this, things can get shifted and out of whack. Maybe most of my days end up being chaotic anyway, but it doesn't affect me. Having this quiet time makes everything seem more controllable, more black and white. I started the routine when I first got married, after Jeannie, who practiced it, suggested I try. I did, but then missed a day here and there, and eventually I wasn't doing it anymore. I returned to it about four years ago, with Jeannie's encouragement. Now I look forward to it every morning, listening to how God will speak to me each day.

My favorite Bible verse is Philippians 4:13—"I can do all things through Christ who strengthens me." That verse gives me the motivation to face challenges every day. It points to how my faith has been a big part of my life. I grew up in the church. When I was nine years old at a vacation Bible school in Washington State, I realized there was something more, something missing. I needed a deeper connection with Christ, so that's when I turned my life over to Him and accepted Him as my savior. It hits people at different times of their lives when they understand the significance of a higher power. Sometimes a tragedy opens their eyes. Sometimes it's a feeling of being lost, kind of like a ship in the middle of the night not knowing where it's going. It hits everybody at different times for different reasons. I'm glad it happened to me at a young age.

My dad was a deacon, and he sang in the choir. We were

always at church. Sunday morning, Sunday night, Wednesday night, youth groups. I was raised in a Lutheran church, and now I'm more nondenominational. I am a Christian, but I don't identify with a specific religion, and my family and I will attend any church where we believe our faith can grow. We all are going to have struggles and disappointments and failures in life, but the one consistent aspect is Christ. Christ is always there. He'll never leave us or forsake us. He's the same yesterday, today, and tomorrow, so that gives me comfort. It shines a different light on everything when you understand that.

People might not like this, but football is not the most important thing in my life. Football is what I do; it's my job. But it doesn't define me even though this world championship has changed how I am perceived. Winning a Super Bowl won't change me. I'm still me. I still want to be grounded and humble. So if I'm having a bad day, I can refocus my attention on Christ. It makes me a better husband, a better father, and a better coach. It helps me deal with conflict at work, maybe something Jeannie and I are going through, or something with our kids. It makes me more aware of what's really important in my life other than football. My relationship with Christ is what my world revolves around.

I don't necessarily preach it to my team. My actions let the team know about my faith. It's the glue that binds and can have an impact on shaping lives. I don't feel this is the forum to do it, but if people ask, I'm happy to talk about it. On Saturday nights at the hotel we have a mass and a chapel service. We do a Bible study for coaches on Friday mornings in season. The players have a Bible study on Thursday nights.

There are times I pray during games. Sometimes I give thanks. I don't say a desperation prayer—"God where are you? Show up. We need you on fourth down." It's more like, "You have this under control, give me confidence, and help me through this. Give me wisdom." It's not about praying for victories—though I have to admit sometimes I do—but more about continuing a conversation.

My priorities in life, in priority order, are faith, family, and football. That means family is more important than the job too. That's one of the things I promised Jeannie when I got into coaching—family would come first. It's especially true in the offseason. When our coaches get a chance to watch one of their kids' ball games or dance recitals or gymnastic meets, I want them to do that. If you miss those things, you don't get those times back.

Shortly after I became head coach of the Eagles, I missed a day of rookie camp to go to my son Josh's graduation from Blue Valley North High School in Overland Park, Kansas. I flew there and back in the same day. It was too important to

ABOVE: Clearly I was ready for some football at a very young age. Cathy is playing tackle while Dad is quarterback.

LEFT: A sign that I was always meant to be an Eagle. Me, in my Ferndale High hoodie.

BELOW: Taking a break during practice with my Northeast Louisiana teammate and brother Craig. I had a good run at Northeast and had hoped that I would get drafted, but that didn't work out.

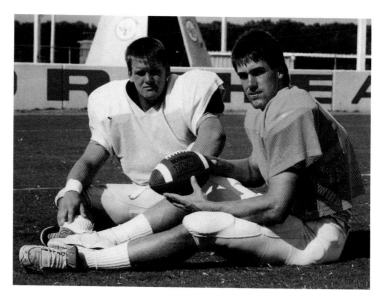

ABOVE: Hanging out after a game with my girlfriend and future wife, Jeannie. We met on a blind date and hit it off right away.

RIGHT: One of the best days of my life—January 18, 1992, the day Jeannie and I were married. She was 22 years old and I was 24.

ABOVE: Here I am with my family. (l–r: David, Mom, Cathy, me, Craig, and Dad.)

LEFT: Dad, in his later years. Gordon was in the Air Force and a deacon in our church. He was a disciplinarian and was tough on us when he coached our sports teams. He passed away in 2016 and never got to share in the excitement of winning the Super Bowl. But I know he was watching from upstairs.

BELOW: My mom, Teresa, and me. Everyone calls her Teri, and she's a social, loving, and tender-hearted soul. If I inherited some of my toughness from my dad, I inherited some of my emotional intelligence from my mom.

The Pederson family—
me, Jeannie, Drew, Joel,
and Josh—before, when
I coached at Calvary
Baptist Academy, and
after, at the Super Bowl.

This is one of my memorable games as a quarterback. With the Miami Dolphins playing against—believe it or not—the Philadelphia Eagles, helping Don Shula win his historic 325th game as head coach. They cut me a month later! The Dolphins were the only team interested in me early in my career, and overall, they cut me five times. That's not a typo. Five.

I was with the Packers for two stretches, 1995–1998 and 2001–2004. I was backup to Brett Favre, and we spent a lot of time talking about the details of the game. And sometimes I played, too. Brett and I became very close and are still friends to this day. But I no longer bring him his Snickers and Coke.

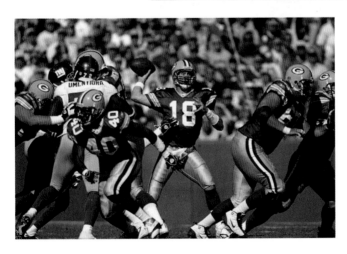

In 1999, I was the starting quarterback for the Philadelphia Eagles. It was a rough year, and I was cut the following offseason for the sixth and last time in my career.

After I retired from football, I coached for four years at Calvary Baptist Academy (2005–2008). It was a tremendous experience being back home with the family in Shreveport, Louisiana. The experience convinced me that I should give coaching in the NFL a shot.

What can I say about Andy Reid?
He's been a huge part of my life,
and as a mentor, he has pushed
me to excel. I played for him
and coached for him (that's
me as offensive coordinator in
Kansas City).

Joining the Eagles meant I would inevitably coach against Reid, who had himself coached in Philadelphia for fourteen years. I was nervous facing him as a head coach for the first time, and sure enough, he beat me.

Quarterback Carson Wentz had a brilliant 2017 season. He helped us get to 11–2 and clinch the NFC East title. When he went down with a torn ACL, everyone was worried, but we rallied. "An individual can make a difference, but a team can make a miracle!" became our motto.

Meeting New England Patriots head coach Bill Belichick before Super Bowl LII.

Nick Foles stood tall for the rest of the season and withstood a tenacious Patriot defense to become the Super Bowl MVP. I was the only NFL coach who visited Nick before the 2012 draft, and we've had a special relationship since then.

Nick Foles scoring on the Philly Special. That was a big play to end the first half of the Super Bowl. But there was a fourth-and-one play later in the game that I thought was much bigger. It was important for us to always be on the attack.

Celebrating with Eagles owner Jeffrey Lurie. He had waited a long time for this moment, as had the Philadelphia fans! It was a thrill for the underdogs to pull one out against the odds.

Here are the 2017 Philadelphia Eagles coaches, players, and staff who made it happen.

The greatest moment of my career—hoisting up the Lombardi trophy.

me. He's only going to graduate once. My son Drew played football at Samford University in Birmingham, Alabama. I was able to go see his spring scrimmage. I also went to his college graduation. We don't need to sacrifice family for this job. We can get our work done. We don't need to sleep in the office and never go home.

In 2017, we were scheduled to play a Monday night game at home on Christmas. The team normally stays in a hotel the night before home games. I took the risk of not having the players and coaches stay in the hotel on Christmas Eve. They could be home, celebrate the holiday, and then wake up at home with their families. We got together later that day and played the Raiders that night. We struggled in that game but won—maybe that was part of the reason. It could have been. But I would not have changed it, even if we lost the game. It's too important. I can't tell you how many players thanked me for allowing them to spend Christmas morning with their loved ones.

Whenever you have a bad day, you still have your family. For me, it starts with Jeannie. We met on a blind date and hit it off right away. We got married in January of 1992 when I was twenty-four and she was twenty-two and in nursing school, and I left to play in the World League the next month. She has been there my whole career, through all the ups and downs. When I was cut six times, she was at my side each and every time. She was with me when we had nothing. The rent for our first apartment was $250 a month, and one month we couldn't come up with the money. We had to use a Discover credit card to pay rent. Back then I was a struggling athlete, but we loved each other and stuck together.

I'm not going to tell you marriage is easy. It takes work. It takes great communication. And it takes devotion to each other no matter what. There are struggles in every relationship. But she's my rock, my source of strength and inspiration. She's everything. She is my biggest critic at times and my biggest supporter. She knows what this business is about. She understands the commitment and the time away.

The best compliment anyone can give me is to compliment my children. I have three amazing sons, and being a dad to Drew, Josh, and Joel is a blessing. To be able to pour yourself into your children and see them grow and spend time with them is so rewarding. I was able to help coach their athletic teams when they were young. Drew is in graduate school at the University of Cincinnati, and I take a lot of pride in how he has matured as a young man. Josh is in college playing football at Louisiana Monroe, and it's great watching him. Joel is in high school, and as he comes up it makes me proud as a father. It's important to be there, at games or just at home for dinner and church together. We also enjoy going hunting together. I was able to teach my oldest two sons how to shoot when we were in Wisconsin playing for the Packers.

I didn't grow up hunting and fishing, but I've always loved the outdoors. I used to snow ski on Mount Baker when I was a kid in Washington. We went camping all the time. Then we moved to Louisiana and I started dating Jeannie. Her dad, George, and two brothers, Jason and Terry, love to hunt and fish. One thing Jeannie said attracted her to me is I didn't do that. Then for Christmas one year she bought me my first shotgun! I had to laugh at that, but it started me on a new hobby, buying fishing rods and reels. Next thing you knew, I bought a rifle for deer hunting, then a couple more. Now I have a collection of shotguns and rifles. One Christmas when my boys were young I bought our two oldest a single-shot .243 rifle and taught them how to safely shoot. Personally, I love to bow hunt.

In college I'd go fishing or hunting—deer, squirrel, rabbit, or dove—with Jeannie's dad. Now in my backyard in New Jersey I have a deer stand set up. I have an electronic feeder that throws out corn, attracting deer all over the place. I've been fortunate enough to shoot a couple of nice whitetail bucks in Wisconsin that I have mounted at my house. Brett and I used to go hunting all the time. We went every Monday afternoon during hunting season, then all day Tuesday. Before daylight savings time kicked in, we could do it on a Friday afternoon after practice.

I also enjoy golf. Jeannie and I enjoy playing with each other and with other couples. We even participate in some tournaments. There are a lot of good courses in the New Jersey area, and I receive invitations all the time. These days, I'm a twelve handicap. When I was playing regularly, I pared it down to a seven. I just don't have the chance to get out much. If I get in twenty-five rounds a year, that's a lot. I bought a golf simulator recently, which comes in handy for working on my swing and feeling the club in my hands.

People probably don't know this about me, but I'm a gadget guy. I bought a drone a couple of years ago, the Phantom 4. I love flying it. I've had it at the Jersey Shore, flying it up above the beach, over the water. I fly it around my house. I've had it at the NovaCare Complex, on the practice field when no one is around. It has a camera on it so you can see everything. It's a great escape. Music, too. I listen to K-Love in my car on my way to and from work. It's contemporary Christian music. I also like the hair bands from the eighties—Def Leppard, Journey, AC/DC, Mötley Crüe. That's my generation's music. In college I got into country, and I still gravitate to that. And if we are sitting around the pool, it's Bruno Mars or Lionel Richie Radio on Pandora. That's what Jeannie likes to listen to.

Something else not many people know is I love working around the house—cutting my own grass, repairing things, doing outdoor projects. I helped with the basement renovation too. I don't mind doing that kind of stuff. My dad was that way, even changing his own engine oil and spark plugs.

We enjoy going to movies too. During the offseason if I have a day off, Jeannie and I will try to catch a matinee before our son Joel gets out of school. I love the Jason Bourne films: *The Bourne Identity*, *The Bourne Supremacy*, *The Bourne Ultimatum*, and *Jason Bourne*. I am a huge action guy. I love the *Fast and Furious* movies too. And because of my weak spot for gadgets, the *Transformers* series is cool. And I am a *Star Wars* guy. I never got into the *Star Trek* thing at all, whether it was the TV shows or the movies. Jeannie is more into the Lifetime, romance-series kind of stuff, the touchy-feely, pull-at-your-heartstrings movies. Jeannie gets on me anytime one of my favorites comes on. She'll say, "Here we go again. You watch the same movies over and over and over." And I'm like, "This is a good movie! My entertainment value, I get it right there."

We like to get out with friends too. I have three really close friends back in Louisiana—Greg Andrews, Brad Burtram, and Kevin Woods. We went to college together, and now they are successful businessmen. We went with them to church and on vacations when our kids were young. We text or talk regularly. They are my accountability partners. We also have some really good friends in New Jersey, people we love hanging out with and going to dinner with.

When we socialize, we often enjoy a good bottle of wine. I was teammates with Steve Bono in Green Bay. He was a veteran player when I was young, and we had a great relationship. Anytime we were on the road we went to dinner together, and he introduced me to wine and sushi. In every city, he knew where to go and where to eat. He's a big red wine drinker. Jeannie and I are probably more Cabernet Sauvignon drinkers. Now we're getting into Merlots and Malbecs. I've never been a real Pinot Noir fan, but we found some we like. And then my friend Dan Laitner is more into the Italian wines. So he is introducing me to some of those. I am trying to expand my palate. In the summertime, we keep a couple of bottles of Chardonnay or Riesling around. On a hot summer night, it's refreshing. I might pour some over ice.

In 2017, we visited Napa for four days. That was one of our bucket-list trips. We had a chance to visit one of Dick Vermeil's wine-tasting rooms. I met Coach Vermeil a couple of years ago, and we have become close. He was kind of a mentor to me during the 2017 season, coaching me along the way. He has been so gracious. Every so often, we get a couple of bottles from him in the mail, and he sent us a case of wine after the Super Bowl win.

Wine is an expensive hobby. Carl Peterson, who worked with Coach Vermeil for the Eagles and later was the general manager of the Philadelphia Stars of the USFL and the Kansas City Chiefs, has a vineyard in Napa. He told me he started out making 250 cases per year, and now he's up to 5,000 cases and they are just starting to break even. I'm learning everything I can about winemaking. The process, from vine to bottle, is fascinating to me. Who knows where it will lead?

I had a wine cellar built in our house recently. We had a sump pump issue in the basement and everything flooded, so we gutted the entire basement and made it more functional. Our son Drew, who is pursuing his masters in architecture, designed our basement. The wine cellar is made of walnut wood with glass panels across the front, along with natural stone archways. It can hold 500 bottles, but I only have about 175 now. It's a work in progress.

Having a healthy, balanced approach to life is important. I'm not one of those coaches who works around the clock. But I still put in a lot of hours. During the regular season, I'm in the office from 5:30 a.m. until 10:30 p.m. or so Mondays, Tuesdays, and Wednesdays. On Thursdays, it lightens up a bit and I'm usually home by 8:30. On Friday, I try to be out by 5:00.

I'm a sound sleeper, but sleeping time is limited during the season. I have to get at least five hours of sleep. I try to get six hours, 11:00 p.m. until 5:00 a.m. In the offseason, I can get between six and eight. Then, after my quiet time, I work out. I ride a Peloton bike for forty-five minutes three times a week and then at least once on the weekend if I can. The other days, I'm in the weight room. I have a dumbbell circuit I do, and some core exercises.

There has been kind of a learning curve on how to manage my time as a head coach. At first I was trying to do everything for everyone. If someone wanted a meeting, I went down right then and did it. If Howie Roseman wanted to meet with me on personnel, I dropped what I was doing. If someone came by my office, I let them in no matter what I had going. All of these people started knocking on my door. Well, two hours later, a good part of my day had just disappeared.

I went the first two weeks on the job and didn't look at any game film from the Eagles' 2015 season because I was being pulled in so many directions. I was dealing with personnel, but I wasn't installing an offense. It became apparent that I needed to manage my time better if I wanted to get everything done. So after a while, I was like, "Time-out, hold on." I had to set up a schedule. "This block of time is Doug Pederson time. This is when we're going to go out there and teach offense. This is when I'll schedule meetings for thirty minutes each."

When you are organized, it's a lot easier to be efficient. So being organized is big for me. You look around, my books are organized, my bottles of water are organized, my files are organized. I'm anal about coaches leaving things around the copy machines—playbooks, papers for players, that kind of thing. And I'm that way at my house. I'm big about if you take it out, put it back. I learned that from my dad, an Air Force guy. In our garage, he had all his tools hung up nice and neat. If we took a hammer out, he made sure we put it back.

When I met Jeannie, she was probably the opposite, a little disorganized. One of the first things I did was reorganize her bedroom at her parents' house. She was still in high school at the time, and her closet was a mess. Everything was piled under her bed or in the closet. So I rearranged everything. Now she's probably more organized than I am. She blames me in an amusing way. Now she can't stand a mess either.

* * *

While I manage my stress well, I do lose my cool sometimes. Not very often, but I can, I have, and I will. Critics may not see me as a Bobby Knight type—someone who is fiery—but that side of me is there. After we lost to the Bengals in 2016, for instance, I publicly questioned our team's effort. I thought it was the right thing to do. I was ridiculed for calling out my players in the media. But I didn't do that. I questioned the entire team, including the coaching staff and myself. I accepted a lot of the blame. I used a lot of words like "we" and "us." I said it was not our best effort. I felt I needed to get the team refocused because we were not performing up to our expectations. If I had to do it all over again, I wouldn't necessarily put it out there publicly and would handle it more internally. But I believe questioning their effort was necessary, and we didn't have a lack of effort after that.

Whatever the circumstances, I try to maintain control and discipline. It's important, though, that players see that passion come out in me at times. When I do get upset at practice or in a game, it's meaningful because I don't do it often. It refocuses the group, and when we aren't performing up to my expectations it becomes necessary.

A lot of people were surprised when they saw the mic'd

up version of our game against the struggling 49ers in 2017. We were sputtering on offense in the first half, and I said, "We better figure this out before I lose my freaking mind." I was pissed. I ripped them that day on the sideline, the entire offense, the players, the coaches, all of them. We were a better team than how we were playing. It's like we just showed up and expected to win the game. I don't roll that way because anybody can beat anybody at this level. I felt we didn't come ready to play, and that's my responsibility too. So part of what I said was directed at myself. I was part of the problem, and I could be part of the solution. We made some adjustments and turned it around in the second half to win the game 33–10.

Against the Raiders on Christmas night in 2017, we were struggling and trying to get some things going. We couldn't complete a ten-yard pass, whether it was because of the quarterback, protection, the route, or play call. Everything was incomplete. I lost my mind. I went off again on the offense. I told them since we couldn't pass it, we were going to run the ball the rest of the game. And I said it in a way that was loud. They got the point, and we figured out a way to win the game. And we did go back to the pass.

In training camp before the 2017 season, we were on field three, practicing a two-minute drive. It was starters versus starters. The offense went three and out. We did it again, and the offense went three and out again. I completely lost it. I went off on all the players and coaches, then stopped the drill and kicked the offense off the field. I had enough. I told them we were not going to win if we didn't practice better. And I used some colorful words that I normally don't use. Fans and media saw it. Some of the media guys picked up on it and made some comments about it.

That's okay, though. Sometimes blowing off a little steam can be good for the team. And for the coach.

CHAPTER 8

EMOTIONAL INTELLIGENCE

When I was preparing to be interviewed for the Eagles' head coach position, I watched Jeffrey Lurie's press conference from the end of the 2015 season. In it, he talks about the importance of emotional intelligence. My agent, Bob LaMonte, and I discussed it, too, as one of the qualities that would make me a good fit for the job. It's all about the importance of having a connection with people and understanding them, of being open, transparent, honest, and direct. Since I became head coach of the Eagles, I have tried to operate with those traits. I want to have a deeper understanding of my team overall, and of individual players and the coaches who comprise it.

Some people might say it's a new-age concept. I think about that, and about some of the history of the game and the coaches who treated their players harshly. Mentally and physically, they'd beat you down, thinking they were making you better through tough, hard practices and verbal abuse. Some of that stuff you can't get away with today. You can't talk to players that way and you can't work that way. Fortunately, there are rules now that we have to abide by. Rules or not, though, I do believe there is a better way of communicating with your team. And we can practice hard too. We can prepare and study and really drive those points home. In addition, you have to show them that you love them and care for them. And genuinely so.

So I thank Mr. Lurie and Bob for bringing the concept to my attention. I've adopted it as my own. I first met Mr. Lurie in 2009 when I came to Philadelphia as an assistant coach. He's an excellent owner, providing every resource we need to do our jobs. I'm very grateful to him for hiring me. It was an honor to be on that podium in our stadium after the NFC Championship Game and hand him the George Halas Trophy, and then to win the Super Bowl and see the joy on his face when he held the Lombardi Trophy.

He's been the owner of this team for twenty-four years.

He's a Boston native, and I think he would have loved to own the Patriots. He has a lot of respect for the Patriots and what they've accomplished, so you could see the weight lifted after we won the Super Bowl. He's as genuine as they come, and we have a great relationship. He can come to me, and I can go to him. There is no hesitation about talking. He has a passion for the city, a passion for his team—and he obviously wants to win, but not to the point where he interferes with the coaches. He lets us coach. That's what he hired us to do. He does like for me to provide him updates on how things are going, to keep him in the loop.

He's in the building a lot, but even when he isn't he tells me he's just a phone call or a text away. We meet once a week in season, usually on Tuesday afternoon or evening. We review the previous game and talk about the upcoming opponent and any injury updates. In the offseason, we connect once a week or every other week. I update him on who's doing what, how we are using certain guys, and bounce things off him. At the end of the year we have a sit-down and he gives me his assessment, evaluating me and holding me accountable for how things went. He allows me to give my ideas, bring up things. It puts things in perspective. If there is an area I can improve, he will steer me in that direction or shed some light.

The most important relationship in the building is

between the general manager and the head coach. Howie Roseman—whose actual title is executive vice president of football operations—and I connected right away. For our relationship to work effectively and efficiently, we have to be on the same page. It's always been a collaborative effort between Howie and me. We have a great dynamic. He won't make a decision without consulting me, and vice versa. This way we both feel there is ownership in the decision-making process. We sometimes watch tape together of a college player or a free agent, and ultimately he pulls the trigger on personnel, but not without consultation. He's all about getting us the best players, and our job is to coach them up and win games.

We're not going to agree on everything. Sometimes as coaches we have a different perspective on our players than the personnel side does because we are around them all the time while they are looking at the tape and the numbers. So we discuss it. Ultimately, we are going to be united on every decision we make, and we all know it has to be in the best interests of the Philadelphia Eagles.

Early during the 2017 season, Howie and I had a discussion about LeGarrette and whether he was getting enough touches to keep him content. I said, "He's going to be fine." I wanted to give it time. Sure enough, it worked out that

LeGarrette was a great asset. Howie told me I was right to be patient, and I appreciated that because he has been running a team a lot longer than I have. When I first came to Philadelphia as a head coach, there was a lot I didn't know. I'm still learning about the salary cap and how things fit and making sure our roster is balanced. He helps me with that. He's sharp and he has a different perspective. During the process of hiring coaches for the 2018 season, I asked him for advice on the types of questions I should ask. When Lane Johnson, our starting right tackle, had a ten-game suspension for performance-enhancing drugs (PEDs), Howie advised me on how to handle that with the media.

After the 2017 season, Howie and I decided I should be more involved in the process of informing players that they were being cut. Since then, I have been involved in some cuts and making some calls with him. It's especially tough with veteran players you have a history with, like cutting long snapper Jon Dorenbos after training camp in 2017 and tight end Brent Celek after the season. Both of them had been Eagles for eleven years. I have a lot of respect for these guys and veterans like them. When I look at projected production, though, I have to be open and honest and tell the player where he is in his career. Older players don't want to hear they can't play anymore. But you can't BS those guys.

It's not easy to disrupt somebody's life. I've been on the other side of that phone call six times and I know how it feels. I wish them the best.

Howie has assembled our excellent scouting department. Joe Douglas, our vice president of player personnel, has a hand in all of our personnel moves. Tom Donahoe, a former general manager in the league, oversees college scouting. Andy Weidl and Dwayne Joseph are on top of things on the pro side. They all work extremely hard to make sure we have the right people and right players in the building with the right attitudes, the right character, and the right makeup to add depth and competition to every position. A lot of credit for the success we've had goes to this group.

I also work closely with Don Smolenski. He sits in on every one of our team meetings and then takes the message back to the people who work on the administrative side of the organization. This way, the people on both the business and football sides are speaking the same language. It's important we have a common language in the building and present a unified front. Don also handles scheduling, communicating with the league office, and fundraisers. We work together on game-day introductions, making sure he knows who the starters will be so they can match the graphics on the video boards.

There are so many people who play vital roles in the

organization that I interact with on a regular basis. Frank Gumienny is our chief financial officer and works closely with Don. He helps bring the team message to his areas. Jason Miller, our senior vice president of operations, oversees the operations of Lincoln Financial Field and the NovaCare Complex, as well as things like the construction of our state-of-the-art draft room. Aileen Dagrosa is our legal counsel, and she advises me on things like issues with an assistant coach's contract or how I should handle doing business with a company that isn't a team sponsor. She's even helped me with how I should phrase things to the team on sensitive issues.

It takes everybody. It takes the marketing team, the ticket office, the people selling the stadium suites, the people who work the Eagles' pro shop, the business department, and accounting. What they do matters. They are a big part of our success, and I want them to feel connected to what we are doing. When you work for the Philadelphia Eagles organization and are out in the community it means something, especially now after winning a world championship. More than ever, people enjoy coming to work, from the chefs in the cafeteria to the receptionist at the front desk.

I remind them to keep the main thing the main thing. We're all here because of the football team. If we didn't have football players, there wouldn't be the Philadelphia Eagles.

We'd be doing something else. So I stress making the team the best we can and remind them that we'll all reap the benefit with more ticket sales, more suite sales, more T-shirt sales, more advertising, more sponsorships, better players, and better coaches.

I appreciate all the work these people do partly because I started out my NFL coaching career on the bottom rung, as the quality-control coach. I assisted the offensive coordinator and worked with the quarterbacks coach. I did a lot of the grunt work behind the scenes that people don't get credit for. It can be a thankless job, working long hours, usually in an inner office with no windows, cranking away. The experience made me value my assistant coaches. They work hard each and every week. And I need them. It is too daunting a task for one man to make all of the decisions. One coach alone can't put together a game plan, so having a collaborative approach where every assistant coach has input is essential.

I set guidelines and parameters for them to work within, but it's important to let assistant coaches have a little freedom. They all know I don't like excessive cursing and yelling on the field, and I expect everyone to hustle from drill to drill. Any of my coaches can give me a good feel for what's going on at his position. I can tell any of them that we need one of his players to perform better. But I have enough to do without standing over them and breathing down their necks. I want them to teach and coach their position without a lot of interference.

Because of my background, I spend a lot of time with Carson and the quarterbacks in the spring, just about every day. But I don't interfere with the drill work unless I see something mechanically with a drop or a release point or their eyes. That's why I hired Press Taylor as quarterbacks coach—to make sure that's right. But I do want Press thinking the same way I think. During the season I'm in the majority of the quarterbacks meetings. It's important they see me in that room and that I have input because I do call the plays. It's important that I get a vibe for what those guys like so I can call those plays during games.

Each offensive coach is given an aspect of the game plan. Jeff Stoutland has the run game—first- and second-down runs, third-down runs, short-yardage runs, and goal-line runs. Eugene Chung, Justin Peelle, T.J. Paganetti, and Duce Staley also are run-games guys. Duce handles screens and quarterback-movement plays, both of which tie into the run game. This way, we can marry up motions, shifts, and formations with whatever we are doing. Justin also handles short-yardage passes and goal-line passes. So he looks at all the third-and-one situations, fourth and one, and anything on the one-yard line. Press Taylor has a hand in the red-zone package. Gunter Brewer and Carson Walch handle some of the third-down situations. Then Mike Groh and I will make sure everything fits, as well as handle most of the passing plays. Ultimately, I make the final call on the game plan. But everybody has ownership. The success of the offense is not about one guy.

The side benefit of doing it this way is that assistant coaches keep growing. As coaches we have to continue to stay up on our craft and keep evolving and finding new and creative ways to keep plays fresh and find new plays. If the coaches feel like the work they do is meaningful and it has success, they are going to work hard because they don't want to fail. After the Super Bowl I promoted three assistants. Mike Groh went from receivers coach to offensive coordinator. Press Taylor went from quality-control coach to quarterbacks coach. Spencer Phillips was my assistant and now is in charge of quality control. I like to promote from within. Those guys have been loyal to me and they know my system. I made a point that I wasn't going to hire an offensive coordinator from outside of this building to replace Frank Reich. Fortunately, I had two coaches on staff who could fill the role—Mike and Duce.

As I said, I'm a big believer in keeping things fresh, fun, and exciting—for coaches and players. For instance, at the start of a week I might tell Nelson Agholor that we're going to run him on a couple of jet sweeps, or we're going to throw a couple of screens to him or put him in some unique formation out of the backfield. When he knows that's in the game plan, he becomes engaged. When the players come in on Wednesday, they want to see if there is something in the game plan for them. If there is, they are going to be juiced all week. I can't design a whole game plan for each guy, but if I have a couple of things for them, they feel like they have more of a stake. They think, "Coach trusts me." I'm fueling them emotionally for the week, and I know they're going to work for me.

I've seen it go the other way too. A player will come in on a Tuesday or Wednesday morning and look at the game plan and say, "Coach, there's really nothing in there for me. Everything is for the other players." So I might tell him we'll add some things on third down or in the red zone to get him involved. But at that point it's already set in his mind. He already thinks that he's not in the game plan for the week. I don't want that.

In training camp, after we've had a couple of good, hard practices together, I'll do something fun at practice or give them a night off. In 2017, I had Fletcher Cox and Jason Peters—two linemen—in a punt-catching competition. Each was given two punts. I told them if both players caught both punts, curfew for the whole team would get pushed back from 11:00 p.m. to midnight. If Peters won, the offense would be allowed to stay up later. If Cox won, the defense would. They each ended up catching both punts, so the whole team won.

We also have a point system with rewards for players. In the spring players earn points for workouts, meetings, and agility drills. At the end of the offseason, we give out rewards like parking places that are closer to the building or a T-shirt—something to make them feel their efforts were recognized. Another way to earn points is through games. We will have a tug-of-war between position groups, or with two or three guys on either side of the rope. It's fun to watch, and the players get into it. Sometimes we'll have what we call a County Fair. We'll set up bags and dummies and then watch the players race, weaving through the obstacles. It's all to promote competition and make us better at every position.

When I was playing, Mike Holmgren and Mike Sherman in Green Bay took the Packers on some fun excursions— paintballing and bowling. One year we had a golf outing. So at the end of our offseason practices in 2017, I took the Eagles paintballing. I wanted them to show up to practice and then surprise them. The buses arrived early and parked out front. All the players were asking about the buses, and they finally got it out of me and ruined it. Still, it was a blast. I had a PowerPoint presentation in which I divided up the players and coaches and named the teams. For about four hours, it was probably the most fun we had outside of winning the Super Bowl. We were covered in paint and mud, and had pizza afterward. There was a driving range and the guys could hit some golf balls. It was a great way to end our offseason program.

Another thing Mike Holmgren used to do was give us vanilla ice cream with all of the toppings the night before our games. I wanted to do the same thing for our players, but I had to fight about it with our team nutritionist, who wanted us to be health conscious. The way I look at it, it's okay for the players to indulge themselves one day a week. So every Saturday night I speak to the team and wrap up by saying we have to watch the highlight video from last week, but let's hurry because the ice cream is melting in the next room. I'm a big ice-cream guy. Häagen-Dazs vanilla ice cream is my favorite, so we have that, along with key lime pie, meringue pie, a fruit pie, and cookies. Many of the guys roll through these desserts.

As a head coach I try to be tolerant of social and political issues. I'm not one to say it has to be my way or the highway. There is too much going on in our world and our society today. These events might not have a direct impact on me, but I have to be sensitive to what is going on, whether it's racial tension, natural disasters, school shootings, whatever it might be. This is the world we live in. And we play a sport that's a game. Everything doesn't hinge on football.

As far as the national anthem goes, I made a statement to our team at the beginning of the 2017 season that everyone would stand for the anthem. I think it's important to our country, and to our men and women who are serving. We had a couple of guys raise their fists. They didn't do it in a spiteful way. They were trying to bring awareness to some of the social injustices they are faced with. We've had a number of outspoken players who have done a lot of good for the city of Philadelphia and the league. As long as they behave in a way that is respectful to the Philadelphia Eagles and that represents their families in a positive way, I'm behind them, and I encourage others on the team to join the fight. Go in the inner cities, help educate, help lead their cause somewhere. Be part of a fundraiser; speak to politicians. Whether it's in Washington or here in Philadelphia or back in their own communities, it's important. If it's about gun violence in school, whatever it may be, get behind it. It's part of the ownership philosophy, putting it on their plates and letting them be men in the community.

One thing you have to be careful about is how social issues can split the team. When I speak to the players in the offseason or training camp I set some ground rules. Try not to bring these things into the locker room. Save it for another time and place—when you are outside of the building, in the community. Our guys have been professional about it. And I avoid talking politics with my players. I visited the White House when we won the Super Bowl with the Packers. Bill Clinton was the president then. I didn't have to agree or disagree with his policies—he was the president of the United States. To be congratulated by him meant something. I have a framed picture of me, a third-string, peon quarterback, shaking his hand. It was a memorable moment.

We didn't have social media back then, but it's something to be concerned about now, so the Philadelphia Eagles have a social media policy. The team monitors all the websites and all the social media sites. I let the players know that they don't need to talk about the team on social media, about how they are being used or played, a scheme, an opponent, or a contract issue. They shouldn't tweet any of that kind of stuff. I want them to stay positive about the team, to never talk negatively. Our guys have been pretty smart with it, sticking mostly to personal stuff, families, things like that. Personally, I stay away from social media. I'm more or less a private guy. I don't feel the need to put anything out there about myself, and I don't care about getting "likes" or accumulating followers.

When it comes to our players, I try to be as accessible as I can be. They all have my cell number and can reach me whenever they need me. I have an open-door policy and I am approachable. I don't care if you are having a bad day or not, you can still be approachable. I have a tighter relationship with my starting quarterback because I call the plays. Carson and I have gotten along very well from the start. We share similar backgrounds and thrive on competition. He was definitely a much better quarterback than I was, but having played the position I can relate to him. He's also a Christian, which was a connecting point. We have a number of meetings during the season, and it's not all about football. We talk about personal things, such as his mission work in Haiti during the offseason and his Audience of One charity foundation, or whatever might be on our minds.

Ultimately, I have a servant heart. I want to serve the players. I want to serve the organization. Whatever I can do to help us be better and to improve, I'll pitch in and we'll build something great together.

CHAPTER 9

CHOPPING WOOD

My first team meeting as a head coach was on a Monday morning at the start of offseason practices in April of 2016. As I sat in my office waiting to go down to the auditorium to address the players, I was thinking, "How can I convince this team that we will win games? How do I get them to buy into my philosophies? How can I get them to believe me?" I had to stand up there, as nervous as I was, and show confidence. Chest up, shoulders back, look them in the eye, and tell them exactly what to expect. It was especially important because we needed to change the culture.

We had to get back to doing things right and trusting each other and building a football team.

I use a three-by-five card for speeches. One of the first things I told them is I don't like to talk for a long period of time, so everything I need to say is on this three-by-five card. As I mentioned earlier, as part of the interview process for the job, Howie Roseman had asked me to tell him and the other executives what I would say in my first team speech. So I started there. I explained the four keys to success: create energy, eliminate distractions, fear nothing, and attack everything. That set the tone as to who I am and how we would get this job done. I told them we would work hard. We would put the pads on in training camp. We would develop their talent.

What I said that day was the beginning of a winning culture that we have established in a short period of time. I felt the message was well received. People said I was like a breath of fresh air, that I was trying to bring some of the joy and excitement back. I wasn't sure about all of that, but I appreciated it. Being a good communicator is essential to being a good coach, and there are different ways to accomplish that.

Quotes are a great shorthand. We hang inspirational quotes on the walls of the NovaCare Complex. One of them, by Will Durant, is, "We are what we repeatedly do ... excellence, then, is not an act, but a habit." He is interpreting Aristotle. The quote is on a door the players pass through every day, reminding them that if we want to be a championship team, then we have to create good habits. We needed to think about developing positive habits in our study, in our diet, in the way we sleep, and in the way we practice.

Another one I really like is on the grease board in my office. "Patience conveys the idea of someone who is tremendously strong and able to withstand all assaults." It is from a book I read, *My Utmost for His Highest,* by Oswald Chambers. That quote, in my humble opinion, captures who I strive to be. I am a patient person. I have been through the wringer. I've heard, "You're not qualified. You have no experience. You have never called plays before." But I stayed calm. I stayed patient. Through patience and through humility come strength, and with it, the ability to lead. And I'll do it alongside the players. That's what I want the players to see every single day, me down there grinding with them and not sitting on a pedestal.

"To be able to withstand all assaults" was a phrase that was especially relevant when we got to the end of the 2017 season. Our quarterback went down, and all of a sudden people were saying we wouldn't win one postseason game, let alone the Super Bowl. My message was to stay patient. Let them pile the garbage on. Let them paint this underdog picture for us. Let's embrace that. Then the next thing you know we were sitting in the Super Bowl against the Patriots, one of the greatest teams in NFL history. And we found a way to win the game.

Another effective way to reinforce the overall message is through a yearly theme. My first year in Philadelphia, the theme was "Chopping Wood." When you visualize chopping a tree, you know you're not going to knock the tree down with one swing. It's going to take swing after swing after swing. The players could easily visualize that. We were going to take some lumps our first year, and quite honestly, we still had some work to do before we could be a great team. But if we kept swinging at the tree, we could eventually bring that tree to the ground. It's one swing at a time, one play at a time—one pass, one tackle, one kick. Just keep at it.

I presented the theme in a team meeting near the start of the season after I had announced that Carson Wentz, a rookie, was going to be the starting quarterback. I am sure some veteran players in the building were thinking, "Oh my gosh, I don't have many more years left. What are we doing with a rookie quarterback?" I'm sure there were a lot of conversations in the locker room too. But I wanted their focus to be simple. Tomorrow will take care of itself. Let's focus on today. Let's start chopping. We started out 3–0, and we were swinging pretty good. And when we lost some games, that's when it really started to resonate with the guys. "Guys, just keep chopping," I'd say. And that attitude was adopted by the team. There really was no quit in our guys that first year. We had one letdown game, against the Bengals. But the other fifteen games were all about swinging. We finished the season with wins against the Giants and Cowboys, so we went into the offseason with a good taste in our mouths. Then we built off that.

Coming into the 2017 season, I knew we had a pretty good football team. In July, right before camp, I did an interview from Lake Tahoe, where I was participating in the American Century Celebrity Golf Championship. John Clark, a sportscaster for NBC10 in Philadelphia, asked if my team reminded me of any other teams. I mentioned the 1996 world champion Green Bay Packers, which I've talked about earlier here, and of course, I was a part of. But I added that in order for us to succeed like the Packers did, we had to have great coaching, great communication, and great leadership. We had to limit injuries and work together. All that was reported was: "Coach Pederson thinks the Eagles can be like the Green Bay Packers world champions."

So now that was out there. I needed to come up with something—one word—that captured the idea that if everyone executed, we could fulfill that. I went around and around. The word "ownership" kept showing up in my readings, TV programs, and on the news. Finally, it hit me. I thought, "Man, that makes a lot of sense." Ownership—let's own this season. Let's own each game. Let's own our jobs. Ownership became our theme.

We have a player council that is comprised of the team leaders. The council is voted on by the team—this way it gives them ownership. In 2017, we had eleven players on the council—Brent Celek, Fletcher Cox, Brandon Graham, Jordan Hicks, Alshon Jeffery, Jason Kelce, Malcolm Jenkins, Chris Maragos, Jason Peters, Darren Sproles, and Carson Wentz. In the first meeting with the council, I told them, "Guys, I'm putting this on you. How do you want this season to go? What kind of team do you guys want to be? How good do you guys want to be? This is in your hands. We will prepare you and we'll practice and we'll do all that. But it's up to you guys. It's about the players. It's not about coaches. It's not about owners. It's not about general managers. It's about players. Players making plays. How do you want this season to go?" Whenever I had a PowerPoint at the end of a team meeting, the last slide simply said, "Ownership." Every day they were seeing ownership, ownership, ownership. As they started believing it, it took on a life of its own. That helped carry us all the way through the season.

My speech at the opening of training camp is part of a meeting where the players also hear from the different departments in the organization and get the big picture. It's about an hour and a half long. The department heads introduce themselves and their staff: "Hey, I'm in marketing." "I'm in public relations." "I'm in ticket sales." "I'm in corporate sales." Our athletic trainer, head equipment manager, video director, and strength coaches also get their turns. Then I speak to them for about twenty minutes with the meat and potatoes for the season. It's our state of the union. By the time I'm done, I hope they understand what is ahead, and what the expectations are. It sets the tone for training camp and for the remainder of the season.

During the course of a regular season week, speeches are part of the routine. On Tuesday, I wrap up the previous game and then focus attention briefly on the upcoming opponent. I might throw out some statistics on the opponent, like how they rank offensively, defensively, or on special teams. It's a general overview. On Wednesday, I drill down further with more specific keys to the game. Usually I present three keys to how we will win the game. The opponent may have a beast of a running back or a defensive end or receiver. Maybe it's the top-rated quarterback in the league. Maybe you are playing an Aaron Rodgers. Containing players like this can be critical. I also go over what we want to do on first and second down.

On Thursday, I focus a little more on situational football. We must win, say, short yardage, or goal line, or third down. All of these vary depending on a team's strengths and weaknesses and how we match up. I don't talk to the team on Fridays. We call them Fast Fridays, where players are in and out by 1:30 p.m.

Saturday morning, I bring the whole week together. We are twenty-four hours from playing, so we really hone in on the game, focusing on our jobs and responsibilities. I might reiterate some specific points or mention a player's insight. At this point I feed more on the emotional side to get them feeling the game.

At the hotel on Saturday night, it's usually like, "What else can I say?" We review and reflect on the week we just came through. I talk about what the weather will be like. For road games, I mention crowd noise to make sure we are prepared for it. I even let them know if the national anthem is before or after the coin toss, so they are ready for everything. Then I close it out with the bit about the ice cream melting and we show a highlight video.

By the time game day arrives, they are ready to play. They don't need another speech from me to get them over the edge or pumped up. A lot of times I let one of the players speak as I leave and walk out on the field.

After a loss, when I address the team I usually put the blame on me... until we get to Tuesday. At that point, after some time has passed and I have done some analysis, I can be more specific about why we lost and I can address some of the reasons. But right after a loss, it's, "I can do a better job. I can prepare you better. I can coach better." I don't want to push blame to the players or assistant coaches, but there are times when I have to say, "We didn't play our best today. You aren't going to tell me they are a better team than we are. We have to get our stuff together."

After a win, we are so excited that I usually provide some perspective, look at the big picture, and remind them that this is one game in the whole. We have to have the same energy, the same emotion the following week. I usually give out a game ball, point out some great plays, and pick some of the highlights of the game. Then we take a knee and do a quick prayer.

Talking to the team can be like talking to your kids. You can say something until you're blue in the face, but it doesn't always sink in. But if somebody else says the same thing, a light bulb clicks on. So sometimes outside speakers can reach the team with important messages. I mentioned Brett Favre's speech before the Super Bowl, and there have been others. Shortly after I became coach of the Eagles, Villanova basketball coach Jay Wright visited the team. He is a lifelong Eagles fan who attends all of our home games and tailgates with his family. I met him when I was an assistant coach with the Eagles, and since I've been the head coach we have gotten to know one another better. We have bounced ideas off each other, and he has helped shape some of my messaging. We have really connected, and I feel honored that someone as accomplished as he is wants to be a part of what we do.

Jay talked about how important the team is to Eagles fans. What it means to them, how they feel like they are a part of the team. They ride high when we win and hurt when we lose. Jay doesn't like to compare what we do to what the military does—after all, we're playing a game, not dealing with life-and-death situations—but he did say we can learn from the military in terms of qualities like leadership, teamwork, and communication. His speech epitomized who he is as a legendary coach and community leader.

Dr. Kevin Elko is someone I mentioned earlier, a leadership specialist and author who speaks to the team four to six times a year. He also helps me with my messaging and thinking, refining my approach to certain issues. He's been a big help in providing direction and making sure my messaging is consistent. Bob Rotella, a sports psychologist who specializes in golfers, has also spoken to the team during training camp.

Athletes are welcome too. When we stayed in LA between West Coast games in 2017, Kobe Bryant visited. Of course he's a Philly native, so he was happy to share his thoughts on having a killer instinct. Everything you do is about that, about destroying your opponent. If you want to win the championship, you have to take care of business each and every day that you come to work. I loved what he said about practice—how the way you practice is the way you play. Brian Dawkins spoke during the postseason. As an executive in Eagles football operations in 2016 and 2017, he was around us a lot. He was involved in scouting, but he also did a great job of counseling some of our rookies. He met with them as a group or spent some one-on-one time with them. He shed some light on what to expect and what it means to be a Philadelphia Eagle. As a Hall of Fame player who played with a lot of passion, he knows what it takes to be successful in this league. He talked about playing in the Eagles' first Super Bowl under Coach Reid. Obviously, they came up short, so he spoke about making the most of our opportunity, remaining intense in practice, and making sure of assignments.

There was inspiration to be found on our team too. Before practice one day as we prepared for the divisional playoff game, Brent Celek and his fellow specialists were out early catching punts and kickoffs. At one point, he called four or five guys over and said, "I've been in this league for eleven years and have never been to the Super Bowl. We have to do everything we can this week, focus on our jobs, focus on our assignments." He brought everything full circle. I was moved. Later, I pulled him aside and asked, "Hey, Brent, would you share with the team what you told the specialists earlier?" He agreed, and it made a difference. After that, I asked other players to speak. I figured the team was tired of hearing me talk all the time, and by the end of the season you run out of things to say.

I thought it would be good to hear from the players who had playoff experience. It had been awhile since the Eagles were in the postseason, so I asked the guys who had been to the Super Bowl—Chris Long, Malcolm Jenkins, Chris Maragos, Torrey Smith, and LeGarrette Blount—to be the last ones to speak. All the players really responded to their perspectives on what this time of year really meant. They talked about one-and-done seasons. They talked about the true definition of "team." Having spent the whole year building up to that moment, it was enlightening to hear those guys speak.

One of the things I've told players repeatedly is I want them to show their personalities. Be who you are. I learned it from Coach Reid, who was always encouraging that. I try to let my own personality show. When we score, I get excited. I pump my fist. I put my hands in the air, I'm high-fiving. Inside, I'm thinking I would love to run and jump and chest bump somebody, but it would be kind of embarrassing.

Jason Kelce certainly showed his personality at our Super Bowl rally. He gave an emotional speech defending many of his teammates. He had heard and read how a lot of us were criticized. He went down the roster, and even mentioned me. An underdog is a hungry dog, he said, perfectly capturing our team. Jason epitomizes the underdog mentality. People have said he's not big enough, not strong enough, so that speech was a release. He had a lot of pent-up emotion from his entire career. I have to say I was surprised his six-feet-three, 295-pound frame fit into that Mummers outfit. But that's him. He was letting it all hang out.

I am not coaching robots. And I don't want them to be me, though often a team takes on the personality of its head coach. If the guys feel that they can be themselves on the football field, whatever it looks like for them, and have fun doing it, that would me happy. Enjoy the moment. Your career is going to last two years or ten years, or somewhere in between. Then it is over. So while you are playing, enjoy it, man. Don't hide. Don't mask anything. Doing that helps cultivate our culture, and if dancing around on the field helps you win games, do it.

You saw some of it in our touchdown celebrations. Taking pretend photos, the line dances, the bowling, the baseball, all that. I'm thrilled when our guys are in the end zone, and I want them to celebrate. It's hard to score. So when we get a touchdown, they should all be there, doing their thing in the end zone. This is not an individual sport. It takes everybody. That's what builds that family bond, that brotherhood, that culture, that excitement around the team. And that's what people talk about during the week.

I mentioned how I have one-on-one meetings with players in my office, often with our quarterbacks Carson and Nick. At the end of the regular season Nick and I had a great meeting. It was the first time since he became a starter that he and I had the opportunity to sit down. He came to ask me about one play. It turned into about forty-five minutes of talking about his journey, his life, and how he and I connected way back in 2012. He shared how he had planned to step away from football a few years ago. He had a lot of things going in his life and his wife was ill, so it was a trying time for him. She is fine now, thank God. We talked about his style of football and some of the plays that he liked. But what stood out more to me was his genuineness, the way he was just being real. It was a conversation we never had even when I coached him in 2012, and it helped me understand him more going into the postseason. For him, it was reassuring to know that he was our guy going forward. I think it helped him.

I have met with Malcolm Jenkins, Fletcher Cox, Chris Maragos, and others too. I have some one-on-one meetings during offseason work, because once you get into training camp and the season, the schedules are more demanding. The one-on-ones establish relationships and allow me to get to know the players a little bit. And they see me in a different light too. I also meet once a week with my player council during the season, on Wednesdays at 8:00 a.m., usually only for five minutes.

Mike Holmgren and Andy Reid always had a player council. It was an excellent way for the head coach to communicate to the team, and vice versa. It's a good resource for me and a way to stay in touch with the team. They didn't have one before I arrived, and during the interview process I fully endorsed the idea. The council brings up a variety of issues. They once told me the players liked the three or four keys to the game, and they asked for further elaboration on them. They felt like it gave them a little perspective and focus during the week of practice. They always bring up the issue of whether players can sit in first class on road trips.

Every year I say no. Those seats are for the coaches. I told them they can sit in first class if they want to come in at 5:30 in the morning and stay until 11:00 at night like the coaches do. We discussed the national anthem in one meeting. After President Trump made some remarks about NFL players, the council elected to stand arm in arm, united for the next game's anthem. And when Lane Johnson was suspended for PEDs, I kept them up to speed on the latest with that. They would be hit with questions from reporters about it, so I provided as much information as I could so they were prepared to talk about it.

At one point early in the 2017 season the media was knocking us, saying the Eagles really weren't as good as their record. So I told the council the team needed to keep doing what it had been doing. They needed to ignore the noise. Lock in and focus. I wanted that message to be spread throughout the locker room, and then I reinforced it myself in meetings.

If someone in that locker room is not pulling their weight, then I want a player from the council to address it and make sure the player gets the message. Sometimes when a coach says something, it goes in one ear and out the other. But when it comes from a peer who says, "Hey, you're hurting our defense. We need you to step up your game. Let's study some tape after practice," it puts ownership on them. They learn how to handle it and make better decisions going forward. This also emphasizes to them that this is their football team, and the ownership is on them.

We once had two veteran players who broke a rule by wearing tinted eyeshields to practice. The only exception we make is when a player has a doctor's notice, but neither had one. So Fletcher Cox went up to them and said, "Hey, what are you doing?" He actually made the players go inside and take them off. Players help maintain the standards, and I'm all for that. In 2017, we had a veteran player who kept messing up his assignments. He was out of position repeatedly for a couple of weeks. Eventually, Malcolm Jenkins went to him during practice and said, "Listen, you've got to start studying. You've got to get yourself right. You're putting the rest of us in jeopardy. We're making up for your errors and it's putting guys out of position." I also saw it in a game where he said, "You've got to own your job. Let's go. Pick it up. Otherwise you won't be out here."

Just because a player is appointed a leader doesn't make him one. For guys like Fletcher and Malcolm, it comes naturally. And that helps create our culture as a team. So even if we acquire a player who might have off-the-field issues, the culture we have surrounds him. He understands he is on a good team with good people, and he doesn't want to be the one who lets everyone down.

As I've said, if a player is late, I'll fine him. But if he's repeatedly late, I'll take it to the council. I'll tell them, "You guys handle it." And that player who has been late straightens up. He gets poked and prodded until he gets in the building on time.

I might use my veteran players to deliver a message, but I try not to use the media to communicate with my team. I don't want my players to read something and ask, "Why is he telling the media that instead of coming to us?" And when I tell reporters something, I try to make sure I tell the team the same thing. I don't air our dirty laundry. It stays in-house. When players are interviewed, I'm glad to see them repeat the messages we drill into them—things like ownership and being where their feet are. That consistency is good for the team.

There are times I have to address specific things publicly. Maybe there is a misconception I have to squash. Maybe a player said something that needed further clarification. Maybe what a player said needed to be supported. In any event, I always go into a press conference with a game plan. It's too important not to be prepared. I spend time before my press conferences making sure I am up to speed on all the potential topics, whether it is a controversial topic or a play-calling issue.

It was Andy Reid who helped me understand the

importance of being prepared and choosing my words carefully. Position coaches don't interact with the media on a regular basis, so dealing with the media was new to me. He coached me up on how to deal with the media here in Philadelphia. Andy doesn't give long answers. That's just the way he is. I tend to be more talkative by nature. But I have to choose my words carefully. When you are a head coach in the National Football League, what you say and how you say it can be a powerful motivator that helps teams win.

CHAPTER 10

MENTORS

I've been fortunate in my life to have been around a lot of gifted people who helped make me the man I am, and the coach I am. My father, Gordon, influenced me as much as anyone. He grew up in Montana and then moved to Ferndale, Washington. He was an all-state football player in high school, and then went into the Air Force. He married my mother while he was in the service, and I was born when he returned to civilian life. He was always a hard worker, a hands-on guy. He worked for Intalco, an aluminum company right on Puget Sound, as a manager. He provided for my mom, me, my older sister, Cathy, and my younger brothers, Craig and David.

He coached all of us in baseball, basketball, and football. Dad would take me to football camps in the summertime. One of them was in Bakersfield, California. We drove the thousand miles to a quarterback camp there, and he was there the whole time. He did everything he could to help us succeed in life.

Dad was a devoted Christian who sang in the church choir, taught Sunday school, ran the youth group, and served as a deacon. We always went to church as a family on Sunday mornings. As I've said, my faith is important to me, and it started here, with my parents showing me the way. It has led me to meet other people of faith in my life. Ralph Paulson was my pastor when I was in high school at First Baptist Church in Ferndale. He genuinely spoke from the heart. When I was in Kansas City, there were two Christian men who had a big influence on me, Dr. Don Brady and Pastor Glenn Shoup. Both helped shape me and taught me how to prioritize what is most important in my life—faith, family, and football. And back in Monroe, Louisiana, Bill Dye and Warren Eckhardt, pastors at North Monroe Baptist Church, have been great mentors. It's amazing to have men like this in my life.

Dad was very firm. When it came to athletics, he was tough on us, pushing us to do extra conditioning and holding us to a higher standard. When I was ten years old, we were at our little league football practice and it had been raining. At some point, he decided I wasn't doing my job. He sent me to the sidelines and made me lie facedown in the mud for the remainder of practice. Later, in my sophomore year of high school, I was on the varsity basketball team and I had a poor game offensively and defensively. We ended up winning the game, but when we got home he only wanted to talk about my subpar performance. It wasn't, "Hey, congratulations on winning the game." It was always about how I could have played better.

That's just the way he was. I look back at it now, and realize how it brought out some of the toughness in me. It shaped my philosophy and how I approached some of the things I do. My aggressiveness and hard-nosed approach are from him. When I have to get on a player or a coach, or yell at an official, I feel there is a part of my dad in me that comes out. But on the other hand, when I had the opportunity to coach my sons, I went the opposite direction at times. I didn't make them lie face down in the mud.

My siblings and I had to walk a fine line. In stores, we had to keep our hands in our pockets so we wouldn't touch anything. If we did touch something, we would get that flick behind the ear—pow! And he had big, strong hands. He was the disciplinarian of the family. My mom, like most moms are, was kind of a pushover. It would always be, "Wait till your father gets home!" And sure enough, if we screwed up during the day, he would give us a spanking after he walked in the door. It was a different time, but the lesson was learned.

My dad was a diabetic, but he controlled it well by taking good care of his body. He always had a treadmill or a bike or something in the house for working out. In 2015, though, he had a stroke and his health began to deteriorate. Near the end, he began to lose his memory because of Alzheimer's. But he would still be able to pull out memories of me playing high school or college football. He and mom came to every one of my games when I played for Northeast Louisiana. During my NFL career, they would come to a lot of the games even though I wasn't starting. It's funny how that disease allows you to recall certain things but forget others. So it was fun to hear him talk about those times, despite the circumstances.

We had just played our last Eagles preseason game in 2016 when we knew the end was near for Dad. It was a busy time. We were making roster cuts on Friday, I had made the decision to start Carson, and I was preparing for my first NFL game as head coach. When my family called to say

Dad was ready to go, I jumped on a plane to Monroe. There were a lot of emotions going on that week. Cathy flew from Wisconsin, and Craig and David were already there. Dad passed about 6:15 at night on September 2,, the day before his seventy-sixth birthday. It was as if he waited until the whole family was there before he passed.

Two days later, I flew back to Philly and focused on our opener against the Browns. It was a difficult period, but football was an escape for me, a way to get my mind off his passing. We didn't have a funeral until the Eagles' bye week, which was the fourth week of the season.

Dad never got to see me as a head coach in the NFL. He would have loved the Super Bowl, celebrating out there on the field with us afterward. That would have been an unforgettable experience for him. Still, he led a good life and now he's in a better place.

My mom, Teresa—everybody calls her Teri—spent the early part of her childhood in Wilson, North Carolina, then moved to Ferndale, Washington. That's where she met my dad. They lived on the same street, just a few houses away, and went to high school together. She was a stay-at-home mom who loved to sew, taking on small jobs. In fact, she has a whole room in her house dedicated to sewing.

When they had a potluck dinner at church, they would ask everyone to cook a dish. Well, Mom would prepare five of them. She still volunteers at church, and has always taken care of whatever we needed.

Of course, that doesn't mean she can't be my harshest critic (it's actually a toss-up between her and Jeannie). She gives me the "What were you thinking?" questions every now and then. She has been around football her whole life, so she understands the game, and sometimes she doesn't understand my decision-making. But as long as it works out, we're good. Mom's a tender-hearted, creative woman who embraces the servant philosophy. She's had a huge influence on me.

My brother Craig was my tight end my senior year at Northeast Louisiana. Now Craig and my other brother, David, referee high school football games on the side. My cousin Rod Brudwick was very influential in my younger years too. He taught me about competition, hard work, and self-motivation. He was a tremendous athlete in high school, a basketball player who would go on to become a very successful businessman and good family man. He passed away in his fifties from cancer, unfortunately, but I'll never forget him.

I had three coaches in high school who had significant impacts on me. Rod's older brother, Rick Brudwick, was a teacher at Ferndale High, and he coached baseball and helped out with football. He helped me a lot with my pitching, and spent more time with me than he did with the other guys. My quarterback coach, Birger Solberg, taught me how to take drops and throw the ball. He really worked with me to develop my talent. He has since passed away, but I received a congratulatory letter from his wife after we won the Super Bowl, which meant a lot to me. Finally, my head football coach at Ferndale was Vic Randall. He piqued my interest in the game and poured himself into teaching all aspects of it.

At Northeast Louisiana, Bob Lane, my quarterbacks coach, took me deeper into the position. He taught me the details of quarterback play, how to read coverages, and how to break down tape. He had some professional experience, playing with the Birmingham Stallions of the USFL, and that informed our conversations. We still talk from time to time. He reported to our head coach, Pat Collins, who reminded me a little of my dad. He was very strict and rule based, and if you even *thought* about messing up, you would be in his office. At times, he would intervene before you made mistakes. He was such a great coach and effective communicator. He would get his guys ready to play. "Be on time when time is involved" is a phrase of his that I still use today with my guys. I stay in touch with Bob and Pat.

One of the great experiences of my football life was playing for Don Shula. I signed with his Dolphins as a rookie free agent and was on and off the team for the next four seasons. He was near the end of his career when I was with him, but he was a legend. I'll always remember the presence he had when he came into a room. When he spoke, people sat up. He didn't say a lot, but what he said was pretty profound a lot of times. He had that way about him. What he said was very black and white and simple to understand, which I try to emulate.

By the time I joined the team, Coach Shula had gotten away from being a hands-on coach. His assistants worked with individuals while he managed the team as an overseer. All great, successful head coaches surround themselves with great assistants—excellent teachers and men of character. Don Shula was no exception. He had Carl Taseff, Larry Seiple, John Sandusky, and Joe Greene on his staff. His son Mike Shula, currently offensive coordinator with the New York Giants, was the quality-control coach my first year. He took me under his wing, coaching me and teaching me the offense. Seeing how Coach Shula put together his staff made me realize the importance of surrounding yourself with good people, and appreciate how valuable assistants are.

I'll never forget walking into St. Thomas University, where the Dolphins held training camp, and seeing Dan

Marino for the first time. I was so intimidated. I idolized Dan growing up. I loved how he played, his aggressiveness, how he was such a fierce competitor who hated to lose. Just the year before, I had been watching him and his teammates on TV. And now here they were: Dan, Mark Duper, Mark Clayton, Jim Jensen, Ferrell Edmunds, John Offerdahl, and Louis Oliver.

When I had a chance to play with Dan, I found out he was everything I thought he was. He was a mentor and teacher to me—not so much with how the offense worked, but more with how to play the quarterback position. He led his teammates in practice the way he led them in games. It could be hard at times, but he made everyone around him better because he didn't care about anything other than winning the game. If you weren't up to par, he'd say, "You're not good enough. Give me this guy over here." He really shaped my perception about what practice is all about. He attacked practice every day, knowing that you win the game during the week, not on Sunday. And it was all about the preparation. There was no substitution for preparation and hard work. Dan Marino and his receivers Mark Duper and Mark Clayton showed that on a daily basis.

Dan was a serious competitor, but off the field he could have his fun. During training camp in 1991, the veterans would make the rookies sing in the cafeteria either at lunch or dinner. I didn't want to do it. So after practice, I would shower quickly, run over to the cafeteria, and leave before any of the vets arrived. I thought I had gotten away with it. Later in camp, Marino came up to me and said, "Hey, I have a buddy of mine who runs this restaurant a couple of blocks up the street. After practice today I'm going to have some appetizers, some drinks. Just hang out a while. Do you want to go?" I said, "Yeah, that would be great." I'm a rookie hanging out with Dan Marino!

So he picked me up in a red, two-door convertible Mercedes. He said it was right off the lot. When we arrived, a couple of the guys were already there having some appetizers and a couple of beers. This is great, I thought. Before long more of the veterans came in. This was a typical restaurant, with couples and families having dinner. But I eventually noticed a stage in the corner with a microphone set up for a band to play. That's odd, I thought.

I put it out of my mind until Dan came up to me and said, "All right, there's your stage. You have to sing for us before we get out of here tonight." Along with everybody else, I had had a couple of beers, so I went up there with my liquid courage and managed to sing "Friends in Low Places" by Garth Brooks. And not just in front of the team, but the entire restaurant. They had a good laugh. Dan finally got me.

In the third week of the preseason in 2017 we played

the Dolphins, and Dan came out for the game. We talked on the field beforehand, especially about quarterbacks. He asked about our process and how we had gone about finding Carson. After all these years, it was great to reconnect with Dan, a Hall of Fame quarterback and a former teammate for whom I have a lot of respect.

I was pretty fortunate to play with another Hall of Fame quarterback, Brett Favre. Of all my NFL teammates, I was closest with Brett. At first he hung out more with Mark Chmura and Frank Winters. But after my first year with the Packers in 1995, Brett and I grew closer every year. Our families were close too: we were at their house quite a bit. One of the things I took from Brett is that you can overcome almost anything when you put your mind to it. It doesn't matter what comes your way, what kind of challenge or what adversity. He had a never- give-up mentality. He played with more injuries than anyone and never once complained about it. You talk about a guy who played for sixty minutes. He played for sixty minutes, hurt or not. And he did it because he loved it.

Brett tweaked his knee against the Redskins one year and sat out the rest of the game, and I played. I went into the training room after the game and he was laid up, wearing a big old knee brace. He told me he would have to have an MRI. I'm thinking, "Gee, he tore his knee up. And it looked pretty bad when it happened." Then he told me we would go hunting in the morning. I said, "Brett, you're in a knee brace. We're not going hunting." He said, "I am going to call you. We're hunting, and you're going." I didn't think there was any way that was going to happen.

So about 5:45 the next morning my phone rang. It was Brett. "Where are you?" he said. I said, "What do you mean, where are you? I'm in bed. Where are you?" He said, "I'm in the tree stand hunting." I said, "How did you get up the tree?" He said, "I climbed up the tree, brace and all. I'm waiting for you."

That's who this guy is. He wasn't going to listen to his doctors, or anybody. He was going to be Brett and do exactly what he wanted to do. So he went hunting that day.

He hated practice but loved games. Everything to him was about competition. He even turned warming up into a competition. We'd start out tossing the ball to each other from ten yards apart, and then it would turn into a game of burnout. He'd throw harder and harder at me, and the next thing you know we were seeing who could catch the hardest throws. And no one could throw harder than he could. I was just trying to catch it away from my face.

Golf was always a competition too. There was nothing relaxing about a round of golf with him. It was, "How close to the pin can we get this one?" Or, "How long can we drive this one?" That's why today I tell my team we want competition at every position. And the only way we can improve as a team and as individuals is through competitive drills.

He always had a way of getting out of trouble while I paid the price. Once, we were hunting on a Monday after a victory in Houston, and I had to leave early to pick up Jeannie at the airport. I was on one end of the property and he was on the other, so I radioed him that I was leaving. When I took the ATV back to where our trucks were parked I noticed these guys standing there wearing orange vests— the game wardens. They congratulated me on the game and then asked if I had heard any shots. There were some poachers in the area. They noticed I had a rifle with me and asked if it was loaded. I told them I didn't know. No excuse. It was. They told me I should have known it was illegal to have a loaded firearm in a vehicle. I apologized and unloaded it. They told me I was in a shotgun-only zone, which I did not know. They were nice about it and let me go without writing a ticket. They gave me a warning, then asked, "Is Brett with you?" I told them he was on his way.

A few minutes later I was in my truck headed to the airport and Brett called, asking who those guys were. I told him, then asked where he was. He said, "I was in my stand. I was watching you with my binoculars. I was laughing my ass off because I knew they were asking about your rifle." I said,

"Yeah. Did you know it was a shotgun zone?" He laughed and said, "Yeah, I did."

I was sometimes the butt of his pranks and his whipping boy. Every day after practice we would have meetings, and every day he would say, "Hey, kid, we need a Snickers bar and a Coke." So I would go get a Snickers bar and a Coke. Mind you, there were rookies he could have made do it, but he enjoyed my doing it. To this day, we still call each other "kid," even when we're texting. That's become our thing over the years.

Packers Head Coach Mike Holmgren always was big on going into a game with the first fifteen plays. And on Saturdays he would ask each of the quarterbacks to come up with our own sequence of plays for the start of the game. Brett would never do one. Instead, he would always tell me to do a second one. He knew Mike probably wasn't going to take any of his plays anyway, so he was like, "Why should I do this? You do it." So I did two, one for me and one for Brett. I felt like I was doing his homework. He loved to have fun, loved to prank people, and he played that way too. He was carefree on the field and kept things light, the epitome of letting your personality show.

Another teammate from my Green Bay days who influenced my life was Don Beebe. We were roommates for a while when I was a young player and he was a veteran. He's a very strong Christian, and a good person. He was someone I wanted to pattern myself after because of the way he led his life and treated people. His work ethic was second to none.

We all benefited from playing for Mike Holmgren. He was another guru of mine. I had a chance to be interviewed by Mike at Super Bowl LII, which was fulfilling and gratifying to me. After playing for the guy, to be able to sit down and do an interview with him on Westwood One about the biggest game of my coaching career was pretty special. Even though Mike called plays, he didn't install the plays other than for the red zone on Fridays. Mike would study and prepare, but he wasn't the late-night guy. He wasn't going to grind. Andy Reid is a grinder. He'll stay there all night. Mike was not that way, and he didn't need to be. So I've kind of taken the Mike Holmgren approach to some extent. I know the areas I need to study and know how to prepare the guys without the late nights.

Talk about a genius. The way Mike could put a game plan together and the way it would unfold during the games was fun to watch. Mike was the epitome of a play caller, and when he was dialed in, it was smooth, rhythmic, flawless. I saw him call a lot of games like that. Mike trusted his feel for the game when he was calling plays, something I've tried to do too. He also shaped my playing career somewhat.

We were finishing up the preseason in 1998, and as we

passed in the hallway at Lambeau Field, he stopped me and said, "Hey, listen. You're a good quarterback and you can play a long time in this league. There is one thing that you need to do that would help you. You need to take your game to the next level. You know the offense and you can function. You can get by doing what you're doing. But you need to elevate. You watch Brett, and he can elevate his play. That's what you need to do."

For me, that meant playing in a little less guarded way. Instead of always taking the checkdown, shoot the ball down the field a little more. Take more risks. Once you make that nice throw through a tight window, it gives you confidence to do it again. And again and again. So what Mike said stuck with me. For the rest of my playing days, I kept trying to find ways to improve my game. Whether it was making better decisions or being a more accurate passer—whatever it might be. As a coach I appreciate what he did. It was an effective way of bringing out the best in a player. Pulling someone aside and investing some time by pointing out that they're good and could even be better can pay dividends. He challenged me to step out of my comfort zone and look at the big picture.

I spent more time with Andy Reid than with any coach, so his influence on me was pretty significant. I had a player-coach relationship with him as well as a coach-to-coach relationship. He has become more of a father figure to me, and I'll always be grateful to him for the coaching career he has helped me build.

We have a relationship that goes beyond football. Jeannie and I have attended his kids' weddings. I was there for him when his son passed away. Jeannie and his wife, Tammy, are close friends. He is a part of who I am. He has shown me the ropes, educated me, and paved the way for me to become a head coach. We had a lot of discussions about game planning, calling plays, running your team, roster building, what to look for in players, working with the personnel department, dealing with the owner—he prepared me for all of it. I was in his office a lot over the years. We had a lot of one-on-one conversations with me asking questions. My coaching philosophy and some of the things I do today with the Philadelphia Eagles are linked to Andy Reid.

He taught me to make the complex simple. Andy's philosophy is the more ways you can simplify things, the better off you are. You know players aren't going to necessarily spend the same amount of time coaches do preparing, so coaches have to try to make it as simple as we can for the players. When the player sees his assignment is easy to understand, he can play freely on game day.

In my entire time as an assistant coach, Andy was the only head coach I worked for. I don't try to emulate him, though. There are some things I do philosophically that are similar. But I am my own person. When I took over as coach of the Eagles, they were calling me Skinny Andy Reid. There are some similarities between us, but at the same time I do things the way I think is best, not the way Andy would do it or Mike Holmgren would do it.

I mentioned Dick Vermeil earlier. He is another former Eagles coach who has helped me. I met him when I was an assistant in Philadelphia, but I really didn't get to know him until I became the head coach. He was one of the first guys who reached out and invited Jeannie and me to come out to his house before my first season. He was out there in the yard with his apron on with the smoker and the grill going, carving up the meal. And we had some of that great wine from his vineyard in Napa. I have a lot of respect for what he did with the Eagles and Chiefs, and for how he won a Super Bowl with the Rams. My impression of him before I knew him was that he was hard nosed. But as we've become friends, I realize he is more of a big teddy bear. He would give you the shirt off his back, a genuine guy. We have friends who say I remind them of Dick Vermeil in the way I handle the team. That's a great compliment.

Coach Vermeil educated me on the media and the fans. He advised me on how to stay on your staff after a big loss or stay after your staff after a big win. We talked about how to refocus the team after a win or a loss. When we had that stretch of games in 2017 when we won nine in a row, he told me I shouldn't back off. He said that was the time to get tougher. I could feel him coaching again, coaching through me. I loved the conversations.

He was gracious enough to share his head coaching manuals from when he was with the Chiefs and Rams. "Hey, listen, make copies or whatever you want," he said. "Maybe there is something in here that you can use with your team." He didn't have to do that. Coaches get kind of paranoid with material like that. I have had a chance to peek at the manuals, and there are some profound things to be found that I can share with the team or just apply in my own life. He has helped shape my philosophy.

He also encouraged me to use analytics. He was into analytics before most coaches were, and he's explained how certain numbers can give you an advantage. He showed me an old report he had on one of his opponents back in the day, and some of the things he had highlighted in there. He also had a colleague run some numbers on our opponent one week. When the report showed up on my desk, Dick said, "You've got to study these numbers. They are everything." And the report was pretty interesting.

Another man who helped me get here is my agent, Bob LaMonte of PSR. He has been a really good friend, someone who works his tail off for me. I mentioned how he helped me prepare for the Eagles' head coach interview. I knew what to expect thanks to him. He and Mark Schiefelbein, a senior executive for PSR, walked me through the process and helped me prepare and get information together.

I met Bob when I was a player in Green Bay. He and Mike Holmgren taught and coached together in California. He started this program called Invest in Yourself. He would come to Green Bay during training camp and do a presentation. Then he went into the agent business and he started representing Mike, and eventually more and more coaches including Andy Reid. So whenever he would come to Philadelphia I would sit with him and we would talk about the glory days in Green Bay.

My first year in Kansas City he asked me if I had repre sentation. I told him I didn't and hadn't since I was a play And I didn't feel I needed one. I didn't want to pay the centage. He said, "Well, just think about it. I wouldn't at some point having a conversation and representin one day." Over time, Jeannie and I felt comfortabl him, so he started representing me. After the 2014 was over he said, "Hey, listen, your name is being c for a couple of head coaching jobs." I said, "I'm Take my name off everything you've got. I'm not ar in He said, "No problem." When the Chiefs had a

015, my name surfaced again. That's when I interviewed with the Eagles.

Bob picks up the phone after a win or loss. We talk about the game, or anything, really. We have built a really good relationship, and he and his wife, Lynn, were with Jeannie in a suite at the Super Bowl.

Bob has had a lot of success and has had some great clients. So one of the things that I am most proud of is that I am one of only three of his clients to ever win a Super Bowl. Mike Holmgren and Jon Gruden are the others. I'd say that's tty special company.

CHAPTER 11

FAILURE

I've talked a lot about the success we had in 2017 with the Eagles. But I've had my share of failures and disappointments too. Everybody who has been around awhile has. It happens. But it's never about being knocked down. It's about getting up. Trust yourself; trust your instincts. Recommit yourself, and rededicate yourself to your purpose. That's how I have handled failures. It can shape your life. I never would have been in a position to coach a Super Bowl winning team if I had not overcome previous failures in my life.

They started early. One of my first big disappointments came in my last football game at Ferndale. We made it to the quarterfinals of the Washington State playoffs as one of the top-ranked teams in the state. A huge snowstorm hit the Pacific Northwest, so our game was moved to the Kingdome in Seattle. That was pretty cool because my family had season tickets to the Seahawks and I was a fan of Jim Zorn, Steve Largent, Curt Warner, and Kenny Easley. I will never forget being on the field at the Kingdome for the first time, my first taste of what the future would hold. I was the quarterback and the kicker my senior year, playing in the biggest game of my life up to that point. I missed a field goal early in the game, though, and we lost 16–15. I felt I let the team down. It was a disappointing way to end our senior year. But I learned the sun still would come up the next day.

When it was time for college, I wanted to go to the University of Washington. I came up a Huskies fan, watching them on Saturdays. I wanted to be at a bigger school— Washington, LSU, Alabama, Ohio State, or Penn State, where I thought it would be great to play in front of ninety thousand people every week. Initially, the University of Washington showed some interest, but then all they offered was a preferred walk-on spot. I was offered scholarships by Idaho and Northeast Louisiana. I chose Northeast Louisiana partially because they had a line of quarterbacks who had come from there, including Bubby Brister, who played fifteen seasons in the NFL. It wasn't my first choice, but it ended up being the best place for me, not only from a football standpoint, but I also met Jeannie there. We raised our family there in the offseasons, and I still have a lot of close friends in Monroe, Louisiana. It is still home to us.

The draft was another disappointment. Back then, in 1991, there were 334 selections in 12 rounds. I had high expectations that I would be picked. I had a pretty good college career, leading my team to the postseason my senior year and setting a lot of records at Northeast. I had 619 passing yards and threw the ball 71 times in one game against Stephen F. Austin State University. I was voted all-conference second team. I wasn't invited to any all-star games, or to the combine, but Dana Bible from the Bengals and a scout from the Bucs came to Monroe and worked me out.

During the draft, I hung out with my family. We had a big ping-pong tournament, hoping the phone would ring. By the time they called the last pick, I didn't know what would happen. But then Jere Stripling, a scout with the Dolphins, called and said, "Hey, Doug, I used to work for Northeast prior to you getting there so I followed your career. We would love for you to come down here to Miami as a free agent. Are you interested?"

The Dolphins were the only team that wanted me, so I signed with them the next week. They gave me a signing bonus of $3,500, and I thought I was the richest guy alive. I always wanted a CD player with speakers, so I bought a five-disc model to enjoy, paid off some of Jeannie's engagement ring, and put the rest in the bank.

It was the beginning of my NFL career, but I didn't exactly follow a smooth path. As I said, I was cut six times, and the first time was that August. Funny story. They were filming the movie *Ace Ventura: Pet Detective* in Miami, and Dan Marino and some of the Dolphins players appeared in it. So Jim Carrey was hanging around camp, and one day I was with a few other guys talking to him when Don Shula walked out on the field. He said, "Hey, Doug, come here a second." I jogged over, and he said, "You know, you're not going to make the football team. But you're more than welcome to come with us to this last preseason game. Or we can send you home today. You just let us know what you want to do."

It took me a second to realize he had cut me right on the field, with Jim Carrey standing there. I knew it was coming, though. All preseason, I had not played, other than a kneeldown at the end of a game. "I think I am going to head home right now if you don't mind," I said. "I'll just pack up and head home." I thought that was the end of my NFL career. I went back to Monroe, and Jeannie and I were married the following January.

I was contacted by the New York/New Jersey Knights

of the World League and thought I would try it out. We played from February through May. After that, the Dolphins re-signed me for the 1992 season. This time, they actually played me a little in training camp, and I had a decent performance. Our backup quarterback, Scott Secules, tore his pec muscle, so he went on injured reserve for the first six weeks of the regular season. As a result, they kept me on the practice squad. So I was on the sideline and traveled with the team. I was like, "Yes!"

But after six weeks, Scott was healthy and they put him back on the active roster. Carl Taseff, the running backs coach, was the "Turk," the person on the team who tells people to grab their playbook and go see Coach. So I brought my playbook to Coach Shula's office, and he told me they were releasing me. I was crushed this time because I felt I had earned the right to be there. I knew I was less experienced than Scott, but to me that wasn't a big deal.

I went back to Monroe again, thinking it was over. A family friend had a Citgo gas station with a convenience store inside and he needed some help, so I went to work for him. I did the inventory, counting all of the items on the shelves and then making a printout of the inventory. If we were running low on an item, we would reorder it. When deliveries came in, I would make sure everything was right and checked everything off the list. It was very Kurt

Warner–esque, and very humbling. I was a former stand-out quarterback at Northeast Louisiana, so everybody knew who I was. But it was what I could do until I got the next call. Or a better job.

I did stay in shape, though, and in the offseason in 1993 the Dolphins called again. I had a really good training camp that year. They ended up keeping Dan Marino and Scott Mitchell on the active roster and putting me on the practice squad. But they gave me a little more money than the usual practice squad salary.

In the fifth game of the season, Dan tore his Achilles tendon in Cleveland. Scott became the starter, and they activated me and I became the number-two quarterback and the holder. So I was getting on the field for all PATs (points after touchdowns) and field goals. It was an exciting time, as I got to play quarterback in a couple of games in relief of Scott too. Then Scott was injured in a game against— believe it or not—the Eagles. I replaced him in the third quarter and did just enough to help the team win 19–14, throwing six times and completing three passes. In fact, it was Coach Shula's historic record-breaking 325th win of all time. We celebrated by carrying him off the field. If you see the highlights of the game, you will see they gave me a game ball, which I somehow lost over the years.

After all that, they signed Steve DeBerg, promoted him

ahead of me, and named him the starter. But the real slap in the face was when they signed Hugh Millen in December. I found out on the evening news I was being cut. We were watching the news, and we were like, "What just happened?" I had no idea. I knew they were working out some guys, but I didn't think I would get cut. It was leaked on a Monday night, and they were planning on calling me in on Tuesday morning to tell me. Coach Shula told me he wanted a quarterback with playoff experience behind Steve, as they believed they were headed to the postseason. I was pissed. I gave him a piece of my mind because of the way they handled it. The best part of it is they didn't win another game the rest of the season after starting out 9–2. They missed the playoffs. So I said, "Yes! The Miami Dolphins, yes!"

So then what did they do? They called me back again the next year. I played well in the preseason, made the roster as the third-string quarterback behind Dan and Bernie Kosar. I was on the roster for the entire 1994 season, but I was inactive every week. I think they felt sorry for me because I had been battered and beaten up.

So for the first four years of my career, the only NFL team that ever showed any interest in me was the Dolphins. Then in the spring of 1995 the NFL held an expansion draft for the Carolina Panthers and Jacksonville Jaguars. Every team listed six players who could be selected, and I was one them. The Panthers picked me in the twenty-second round with the forty-fourth selection. They also selected another quarterback right after me, Jack Trudeau, who had started a lot of games for the Colts and had played for the Jets. And they signed Frank Reich as a free agent.

I went through the whole offseason in Carolina. Jeannie and I leased an apartment there. When they drafted Kerry Collins from Penn State in the first round, giving us four quarterbacks, the writing was on the wall. I looked around and knew. Trudeau was a veteran. Frank had just come from the Bills, where he was with the Panthers' general manager, Bill Polian. Everyone thought he would be the starter. And then Collins was the draft pick. I was the odd man out. They would have to guarantee my salary if I was on the roster after June 1, so they cut me at the end of May. We packed up and drove back to Monroe.

I signed with the Rhein Fire of the World League for three weeks. I lived in Dusseldorf, and it was a great experience. We had to take a train to practice every day from the hotel. There was this one restaurant that made these unbelievable brick-oven pizzas. Then who called? The Dolphins.

So I re-signed with them for the fifth time. They also signed Dan McGwire, Mark McGwire's younger brother, a big, tall dude with a pretty decent arm. I played really well that preseason when I had the chance. At least I felt I played a lot better than he did. And if the team had a vote, they probably would have made me the third-string quarterback. But they had invested more money in McGwire, who was a former first-round pick. They cut me at the end of camp.

When I met with Coach Shula, I was exhausted by it all. "Listen, I think it's over," I said. "I appreciate everything you guys have done for me. But this is probably the last straw." At that point, I was thinking my playing career was over. I told Jeannie I was done, and that I was coming back home to find some work. I have an undergraduate degree in business management, and I figured I could find something and we would live happily ever after. But really, it was a low point in my life. Back home I worked for RPS—Roadway Packaging Service—which was like United Parcel Service. I was the jumper in the car, meaning I was the guy who would run out and drop off the box when the driver, Craig Bryan, would pull up. I did that in September and October of 1995.

Then one day I was delivering packages and the home phone was ringing off the hook. The Green Bay Packers, New York Jets, and Oakland Raiders all called on the same day. All three teams had quarterback injuries, and all of them told Jeannie that they wanted me to work out for them. She told them she would track me down. We didn't have cell phones back then, so she called the businesses along our route until she reached a guy who worked at Chef Hans'

Gourmet Foods, which is a Cajun spice company. When I walked in to make the delivery, they told me I needed to call home. Jeannie told me the exciting news. I immediately set up a trip to Green Bay first, then to New York, and then a few days later to Oakland.

I had not touched a football for two months and I hadn't been working out because I thought my football career was over. But when I worked out for the Packers, I don't think I missed a throw. Mike Holmgren, Steve Mariucci, and Marty Mornhinweg were there. Every ball that came out of my hand was a tight spiral. I was on point. I was amazed at how well I was throwing.

The Packers weren't ready to make a move, so from there I went to work out for the Jets. My workout wasn't the same. The balls were a little loose. I just didn't feel it that day. So I flew back to Monroe, and while I was in the air the Packers called the house and talked to Jeannie. When I landed they said they wanted me to cancel my trip to the Raiders and sign with them in two weeks. I was relieved, to say the least. So I stopped working for RPS and started working out. Sure enough, they signed me to the practice squad with five weeks left in the regular season. We made it all the way to the NFC Championship Game that year and lost to the Cowboys.

They signed me through the 1998 season, and I became

the third-string guy behind Brett Favre and Jim McMahon. We made it to the Super Bowl after the 1996 season and then again the next season. After the 1998 season we lost in the wildcard round to San Francisco 30–27. Then I signed with the Eagles as a free agent.

I played in Philly for one year, and then I was cut for the sixth and final time. In 1999 I came in as the starter. It was Andy's first year, and he had to make some tough decisions with the roster. He let a bunch of the players go and started bringing in his own guys. We weren't very good as a team. But we did have fun playing together.

One year later, I was supposed to be the backup to Donovan McNabb in his second season. Before the fourth preseason game, Andy Reid came to me and said, "I'm not going to play you at quarterback in this game." I asked why, and he said he wanted to let the young guys play. By then, I knew how everything worked. Then the next day Jeannie and my kids and I were with Vince and Janet Papale at their pool. My phone rang. It was Andy. "We would like for you to take a pay cut to free up some cap space," he said. "No, I'm good," I said. "I signed a deal last year and I think the team should honor the deal." He answered that either I had to take a pay cut or they had to let me go. I said, "Just let me go then; cut me." And so he cut me after training camp in 2000, and they kept Donovan and Koy Detmer.

I was so mad. I was mad at Andy. I was mad at the game. I was done with football. I felt it was unfair. I was being cut for something that had nothing to do with my performance. I worked my tail off to get there, and I had been cut so many times, and I said, "Dang, when can you ever catch a break in this game?"

Cleveland wanted me to sign with them right away, but I wasn't interested in playing anymore. Andy kept calling and tried to convince me to go to Cleveland. I said, "No, I ain't going. They all can kiss my tail. I am done with football. It's over." But I slept on it. Then I had a really good conversation with Chris Palmer, who was their head coach. He said they needed a veteran guy behind Tim Couch, the first pick in the draft, and he would love to have me. So we packed up our belongings in a U-Haul trailer and drove all the way from Philly to Cleveland with a one-year deal for 2000. But my heart really wasn't in it. I was like, "What am I doing? This is so dumb. I'm moving my family again for what?"

Before our eighth game, Tim Couch broke his thumb in a practice late in the week. I had one day to practice to be the starter, and then we flew out to Pittsburgh. I threw three picks and we were beat 22–0. We were crushed. It was awful.

I ended up starting seven more games that year, and the Browns had a 3–13 season. My one victory as a starter that year came against the Patriots and Bill Belichick. So now I've beaten him twice. We had several starters on injured reserve—and they were an expansion team the year before. We played with a lot of rookies, and a lot of journeymen, including myself. Our last game that year, Jim Schwartz, our defensive coordinator in Philly, was with the Tennessee Titans, and they came to Cleveland with Steve McNair and Eddie George and all those guys. They had a playoff team and beat us 24–0 in a driving snowstorm. We had one foot in the parking lot. I was playing with broken ribs, and we had nobody left to play. It was not my best NFL experience. I became good friends with Phil Dawson, the kicker for the Browns, and he made it a little easier to go to work every day.

At the end of the season, Chris Palmer was fired and my contract was up, so I was out of work again. Matt Hassel-beck had just left the Packers to go to Seattle, so the Packers called and said they needed a veteran guy. I went back to Green Bay and played four more seasons before retiring. By the time I was finished playing, I had a 3–14 record as a starter. Somebody told me that's the fifth-worst percentage in NFL history by a quarterback who started at least fifteen games. It shows you how hard it is to win in this league.

Even though I didn't have a lot of individual success, I feel blessed to have played fourteen seasons in this league. Some people might look at my playing career as disappointing, but

I didn't. To have developed the relationships I did, to play with some of the Hall of Fame players who I played with, to learn from them—it was a great experience. I mean, I won a Super Bowl with Green Bay, and was the quarterback for Don Shula's 325th win. I was the holder on Thanksgiving Day in Dallas when the Dolphins beat the Cowboys 16–14—the famous Leon Lett game. We lined up for a field goal to win the game with fifteen seconds left. I held the ball, Pete Stoyanovich kicked it, but it was blocked. The ball rolled toward our end zone, so we all chased after it to try to jump on it. It was raining and sleeting, and the surface was slick. And here came Leon Lett. He tried to scoop it and instead pushed it closer to our goal line. We ended up recovering on the one-yard line. So after the referees reviewed everything, we lined back up with three seconds left and kicked the game-winning field goal. That's a good memory.

There have been some games in my coaching career that we lost that have stuck with me. In 2007, when I was the head coach of Calvary Baptist, we had a really good team and were highly ranked. We played a game against St. James at their place on a Friday night, and if we won the game we would have played for the state championship. They had a lot of speed on defense, and I told my quarterback all week that he would have to throw before the receiver came open. I set up drills for him to anticipate, and I felt really good going into the game. We took the lead in the third quarter. But he missed a couple of wide-open guys in the end zone. He became hesitant on throws, and we ended up getting beat. Afterward, I felt I could have done a better job preparing the team. I was working with my quarterback to make throws, but I wasn't reinforcing that the entire team needed to play for four quarters.

Another loss that was hard to get over was in the 2013 postseason. I was the offensive coordinator for the Chiefs, and we were playing the Colts. We went up 38–10 early in the third quarter. And then everything that was going right for us started going wrong. They came back to beat us 45–44. It was so disappointing. We had a good team, but we didn't finish the season the way we started. Learning how to finish is so important. It goes back to my theme for the Eagles in my first year as head coach: chopping wood. You've got to swing for four quarters, something we didn't always do my first year as head coach with the Eagles. There were some losses that might have been the result of a poor call from me, or a late turnover, or a penalty—something that kept the drive alive for our opponent. Like our overtime loss to the Cowboys where we allowed them to tie in the fourth quarter. It's hard to get over things like that, but it just goes back to how you bounce back after getting knocked down.

When I have experienced these disappointments, my

faith and my family helped me keep perspective. You have to rely on Christ and trust in Him in everything you do. If you stay faithful, you don't have to reinvent the process. Being grounded in my faith helps me. I know if I just keep plugging away, swinging away, chopping wood, I will be fine.

Jeannie knows when I am down. She sometimes believes in me more than I believe in myself. She always expresses confidence in me. And as much as I haven't wanted to hear it at times, her perspective has been good for me to hear during some of the tough times—especially since I've been a head coach.

When you are the head coach, it's just you, and everyone else kind of scatters like crickets when the lights come on. They find places to hide. You are the only one out there. So it's good to have someone supporting you no matter what happens. Jeannie is always there, encouraging me to keep the faith, stay the course, and trust the process. She has really helped me through the tough times throughout my career.

CHAPTER 12

STAYING THE COURSE

Sometimes, it's hard for me to believe that I played fourteen seasons in the National Football League, and now I've been coaching for another nine. There are a lot of reasons why some people last in this league. For me, a part of it is my commitment to staying the course.

When a guy is cut once, he often has a hard time making it back—let alone making it back after being cut two or three times. I wasn't even drafted in the first place, and being cut as many times as I was, as I look back on it, God truly had a hand on my career for me for a higher purpose. He totally, completely blessed my career of fourteen years.

And I never once dreamt that a kid out of Ferndale, Washington, was ever going to play for that long in the National Football League or become a head coach. When I reflect on it, I can see that resiliency has been part of my fabric. You could say that resiliency was a defining quality of the 2017 Eagles as well.

There were times in my career when I was frustrated about not playing. There were definitely times I was frustrated about being cut, and how I felt the system hadn't been fair. I thought about quitting at times. But it was never really an option—it's the easy way out.

Even when I was set to be the starter for the Eagles in the summer of 1999, I had thoughts about quitting. It was Andy Reid's first training camp—the hardest and hottest camp ever. We were in pads the entire camp, hitting all the time. Life was miserable. But I survived, and it got better from there.

I was disappointed the next training camp, too, when Andy promoted Donovan McNabb to start ahead of me. I knew the Eagles had to play their first-round pick, but as an athlete, pride takes over a little bit, and you say, "I should be the one who's starting." I wanted another chance to lead this team.

I've been called a career backup. It fits. I'm okay with people saying that about me. Or they can say I was a journeyman. You can call it what you want, because I had a good career. There are starters and there are backups and there are role-players. My role was a backup, to provide support. It was about being a servant and serving others. I understood that and I embraced it.

Sometimes being a backup is nerve wracking. Sometimes it's the best job in football. For the most part, you are going to stay healthy, and you are going to accrue seasons in the National Football League. So it's a great way to make a living. You just have to be comfortable with not playing much and with having to prove yourself every year.

I have talked to my players about it, why it's important to accept a role and understand what is expected of them. There were players on our Super Bowl team who came into the league the same way I did. Trey Burton and Rodney McLeod were undrafted free agents, and these guys are well into their careers now. They weren't cut as many times as I was, but it's fun to watch them take off because I know what they have been through.

There is an art to surviving in the NFL, especially as a backup. It helps to have the ability and willingness to communicate with your coaches. You need to be reliable and stable. You need to be the type of person who is going to do the right thing, show up on time, and be a good teammate. All of that is part of lasting fourteen years. If a coach thinks,

"Hey, we can trust this guy," he is going to want to keep him around.

Later in my career, it was a plus that coaches saw me as being good for Brett. I never resented being thought of as Brett's guy. It goes back to when you get older in this league, you have to learn to adapt. It was genuine, though, not fake or phony, and I think that's what people saw. I hope that's what they saw, anyway. I truly believe I was able to help Brett be a better quarterback. I look back at my career and I think that's why God placed me in Green Bay and brought me back to Green Bay—to help and support Brett and do whatever I could to help the team win.

There was a trust between us. Brett, especially earlier in his career, wasn't the most detailed guy in the world. I was the other way. As he got older, he became more detailed and I was another set of eyes on the field for him, which would allow us to review things in meetings. I don't want to say I coached him up, but we had conversations that I think were beneficial. We might talk about an opponent, a play, or a protection. My deal as a backup was to study the protections and understand the fronts and coverages. He could come to the sideline from the field and we could talk about what we were seeing. Whether it was in-game or during the week, I provided the information to him that was necessary to help win the game.

I always liked to chart the games. I would chart the down and distance. I would chart the personnel we were in. I would chart the defense. I studied defensive coordinators' hand signals back in the days before they could talk directly to the linebacker through the headset. And I would write out whatever he was doing. After about the third series of the game, I would have all the hand signals down. I had a headset, and once our quarterbacks coach, Darrell Bevell, told Brett the play, I told him what to expect from the defense.

It was a big help to us offensively, obviously. I could tell him when a blitz was coming, or what coverage, whatever it might be, based on the charting. It was all about trying to gain the competitive advantage.

I also studied the defensive coordinator's body language. If he had his hands on his knees or was acting nervous by, say, pacing, that was usually another clue that something was coming—maybe a blitz. So I told Brett to look for it, and he could make a check or alert his line, as well as have a plan for where he was going to go with the football.

I tried to help our defense, too, by presenting the right picture in practice. Part of my role as the backup was playing the opponent's quarterback. I would review film of the opposing offense, watching for the mannerisms of the quarterback. Sometimes I watched a TV tape and listened for the opposing quarterback's cadence, anything that would help me imitate him for our defense. I would even grab some of our young receivers, along with the practice-squad guys, and have them watch some film of the opposing offense during lunch for maybe ten minutes. This way we could get some route combinations to show the defense.

I still was trying to develop my talent and prepare myself in case I needed to play on Sunday, but I put a lot of effort into preparing the defense. I took it very seriously. My mentality was, "How can I beat our starting defense?" Sometimes someone like LeRoy Butler would come to me and say, "On this play we were trying to put a disguise on. Could you tell what coverage we were in?" I would give him some feedback on how wide they were off the hash, or where his eyes were, or something like that.

I still preach the value of scout-team work today as a head coach. You can be a big part of your team's success on Sundays by giving a good picture in practice. Jim Schwartz will ask Nick Foles or Nate Sudfeld certain questions about a defense. Or he might ask if they could sniff a blitz, or if their disguise was effective. As you get older in this league, it's not always about making contributions as an athlete. Sometimes it's about helping your team in other ways, even if they're simple.

As my career progressed, I had some advantages as a

wily, seasoned veteran. I knew how everything worked and how to approach training camp so things might go in my favor. I could use the knowledge I had built up in a certain way that allowed me an upper hand against the competition that was trying to beat me out.

But I also felt an obligation to help teach, to help bring a quarterback along, to show a tight end how to run a route. During the later years of my career, especially the last couple, the coaching juices started flowing. The Packers had Craig Nall as our third-string quarterback, and I was coaching him up on certain things. The longer I was in the league, the more I took on that type of role.

As I aged, it also became easier for me mentally but more difficult physically. I couldn't take a month off after the season like I did when I was younger, because my body wouldn't bounce back the way it used to. Each year that went by, it seemed like I had to start training in the offseason sooner. So I'd go back to Louisiana and work out every day.

Then I had to start throwing before the first minicamp to get my arm back in shape. Conditioning was important because Brett would attend but wouldn't practice, which meant I was in for a ton of reps. That was big for me, going in there at thirty-five or thirty-six years old and showing them that they could trust me.

Early in my career, I learned the more I could do for a

team, the better it was for my survival. I became a holder in 1993. When Dan Marino had a season-ending injury, Scott Mitchell was promoted to replace him as the starting quarterback. He wasn't going to hold anymore, so I took over holding for Pete Stoyanovich.

My first hold was an extra point against the Kansas City Chiefs in Joe Robbie Stadium. I dropped the snap and yelled, "Fire!" That let everybody know there would be no kick attempt, and I would try to get the ball across the goal line. I spun out to my right and tried to throw a pass into the back corner of the end zone. I got lit up. I was so embarrassed. It was my first time out there, and I was a little nervous, so I took my eye off the ball.

My first couple of years in Green Bay, Craig Hentrich, our punter, was doing the holding. After he left for Tennessee I became the holder, and I held for the remainder of my career. I held for Ryan Longwell in Green Bay, then for David Akers and Norm Johnson in Philadelphia, and Phil Dawson in Cleveland. I was a holder for more than seven seasons. I took pride in it and worked on it every single day on the field. I enjoyed it until it was minus-8 degrees out there at Lambeau Field and I had been sitting on the sideline for a while. I was stiff and had to go out there and put the ball down.

My son Drew was the quarterback and holder at Samford, so I'm partial to that position now. You don't see too many quarterbacks doing it anymore, usually because it's easier for the punter to do it. He is always with the kicker. But for me, it was an opportunity to have an impact on the success of the team.

During my first stay in Green Bay, I started using my thumb and my pointer finger at the top of the ball on holds—it's called the pinch technique. Most holders use just one finger, but this gave me more control and I could spin the ball with one hand, as opposed to trying to do it with my free hand. It didn't really get noticed until 1999 in Philadelphia when John Harbaugh was the special teams coordinator. He asked me about it, and when he became the head coach in Baltimore, he began teaching the technique. So I have been anointed the father of the pinch technique. More and more guys have gone to it.

I was a part of some pretty cool things over fourteen seasons in the league. I will never forget playing the Cowboys in the old Texas Stadium with the hole in the roof. I got to play in all the great old stadiums. I was fortunate to play in Lambeau Field, that historic football site. I was able to understand the history of the team, from the Acme Packers' days back in the 1920s. It was an honor to play there.

I have some good memories of Veterans Stadium in Philadelphia. We would come out on the first-base dugout side onto the field, and that turf was terrible. They had the old Liberty Bell up in the corner of the stadium. We practiced there every day. In the locker room we would hear cats chasing mice and rats in the ceiling. Coaches would tell you stories about coming in the office in the morning and seeing the animals' droppings that had fallen through the ceiling. Our meeting rooms were on one side of the concourse and our locker room was on the other side, so you had to cross the concourse. If you weren't careful, you could get hit with a forklift or service truck ripping through there. You literally had to look both ways and make sure nothing was coming. It was a mess. We had a practice bubble that was about as big as my office. Those are some fond memories, though.

I had a chance to play in the old Memorial Stadium in Cleveland and the old stadium in Baltimore where the Colts used to play, which also was called Memorial Stadium. I played in the Kingdome in Seattle as a pro before they blew it up, and I remembered my high school game there. The Oakland Coliseum is another one—I loved playing in that stadium. I know it's old, but there is something about going into that stadium with the Black Hole. Both teams enter from the same tunnel and split from there. The Murph in San Diego was another great stadium to play in before the Chargers moved.

I loved going to the old Soldier Field in Chicago when

I was in Green Bay. To play in that stadium and feel the aura and remember some of the great games and players who played there—Walter Payton, Jim McMahon, and that great Bears defense—that was something. And then I loved visiting the city. We would try to get there early enough to grab dinner. Christmastime there was amazing, when they had the city decorated and you could do a little Christmas shopping.

Getting to play in places like that was a privilege that had to be earned every year. I felt like I had to do a job interview every season. Of the fourteen seasons I was in the NFL as a player, I'd say I was confident that I had a roster spot in preseason in six of them. In the other eight seasons, I was competing for a job. A lot of times, it was against a former first-round pick. I mentioned Dan McGwire in Miami. In Green Bay, they brought in Akili Smith one year. At different points, they brought in Rick Mirer, David Klingler, and Tim Couch to compete in Green Bay.

When they sign guys like that, the first thing is you are a little agitated, and you are miffed. Then you go, "All right, I got it." Competition. Iron sharpens iron. That's what I preach today. Bring in competition at every spot and embrace it. That kind of competition made me better and tougher. It made me own my job. It made me study, and it made me prepare.

Playing in the National Football League was a dream of mine, and I didn't want that dream to go away. So I did whatever it took to fight and scratch and claw and make that roster. I just stayed the course and did what I always had done. I knew once the season started in Green Bay, Brett was going to go in and I wasn't going to play. So I approached training camp as if it were my regular season. I gave it everything.

The advantage I had over those guys in Green Bay, my secret weapon, was the fact that I was familiar with the offense and they weren't. I knew the details, the ins and outs. I could execute that offense at a high level, and that showed them I was capable of continuing as the backup to Brett.

Some of those guys had more talent than I did. There were some days when I was sitting there thinking, "Wow, this might be the year I get released and they keep this guy." But then you put on the pads and start playing games. That's when it became apparent why I was there. Sometimes the guys with great arm talent and athleticism aren't the best quarterbacks in the moments when you really need them.

I wasn't intimidated by the fact those guys were high draft picks. After I was around most of them, it was like, "Are you kidding me? This guy was a first-round pick? What is so special about him?" Maybe he threw for a lot of yards or played in a big bowl game. That was the pride in me, I guess.

That's why even today when I am studying players, I look for guys who have flown under the radar but who have a great work ethic and are hungry—guys who remind me a little of myself as a player.

We have a couple of them on our roster who are like that. One is Nick Foles. He was under the radar in the draft. After all, I was the only coach who had worked him out. Another is Halapoulivaati Vaitai—Big V as we call him, the offensive tackle from TCU. The gurus out there weren't talking about this guy in the mock drafts. But I kept studying him. He had great feet and pretty good hands, and needed to work on his balance a little. So we drafted him in my first year with the Eagles, and started working with him. He wound up starting his rookie year at right tackle when Lane Johnson was suspended. And in 2017 when Jason Peters went down, he moved to left tackle and had an outstanding season. I love everything about the kid. He's a special player. He works hard, he's quiet, and he's a detail guy.

If you are going to last as an NFL player, you have to learn to play hurt. Even though I didn't play a lot, I had to fight through some injuries. I broke my jaw and I cracked my ribs twice. My last year, I fractured the transverse process in my spine.

I took some other pretty big hits. In 1992, when I was in the World League playing for the New York/New Jersey

Knights, we were playing the Frankfurt Galaxy in Germany. I dropped back to pass and got nailed in the back. This was before I had LASIK surgery, so I was wearing contacts and was hit so hard that they were knocked out of my eyes. I was kind of freaking out because I couldn't see a thing.

When I was playing for the Eagles we went against the Bucs when they had Warren Sapp, John Lynch, Derrick Brooks, and all those guys. I dropped back to pass and Brad Culpepper hit me low, and then Sapp came over the top. They folded me up like a lawn chair. That one hurt.

I was pretty lucky overall, though. Aside from some tendinitis in my elbow, and some arthritis in my knee and shoulder, I don't have many other aches and pains from my playing days. I didn't have any concussions that I knew of. Back then, concussions weren't diagnosed the way they are today. I did get hit many times and stood up not really sure of where I was. I shook it off and kept playing. That's just what we did.

The league has come a long way with concussions. The referees are on top of it, and the spotter in the press box is all over it. I think the new technology helps with better helmets to protect the head. I am all for player safety because our business is about players. I'm an advocate for anything that can reduce the number of concussions. I don't think we can ever eliminate them—it's just the nature of the game—but the system we have is working well.

All three of my sons played football, and it wasn't an issue in our house. Football players know exactly what they are getting into, and concussions are an acknowledged part of the game.

The game has been good to me and my family. But it wasn't difficult to walk away after the 2004 season. Jeannie and I took a trip to Mexico with Phil Dawson and his wife, Shannon, and it was a week of soul searching. We prayed about the decision to retire, and if I should start coaching high school football at Calvary Baptist Academy. Jeannie and I agreed to talk to them and see what the job entailed. It worked out well.

I could have continued to back up Brett, tried to squeeze another year out of it. But I was about to be thirty-seven years old. They ended up drafting Aaron Rodgers that spring, so I probably would have been the odd man out anyway. Bottom line, it was time. I had been moving my family back and forth from Monroe to Green Bay. My kids were getting older. It was time to settle down a little bit, have more of a normal life.

I was born too early to make a ton of money in my playing career. My best year was 1999. Between a $3 million signing bonus and a $700,000 base salary, I made $3.7 million that year. That was as a starting quarterback in the league. They are making a little more than that these days.

I don't think I could have become the coach I am without my playing career. There are a lot of guys out there who are great play callers who probably haven't played the quarterback position. But for me, a lot of it is about the feel of the game, seeing it through the eyes of the quarterback, standing there behind the center, taking the snap, dropping back, and reading the defense. I prepare during the week just as if I'm playing.

Then I take our quarterback's strengths, tie it in to the game plan, and make all the pieces work. That's the fun part. It's being Carson Wentz or being Nick Foles and seeing it through his eyes.

Being a former player is helpful for any coach. Six of the coaches on my 2017 staff had pretty good careers in the National Football League. Frank Reich played quarterback in the NFL for a long time. My former teammate Duce Staley is my running backs coach. Justin Peelle coaches tight ends, a position he played in the league for ten years. Eugene Chung is the assistant offensive line coach and a former teammate. Phillip Daniels is the assistant defensive line coach. Tim Hauck is the safeties coach and another former teammate. And then a lot of guys played college football.

They are better able to see things through the eyes of their players.

Consistency is important in coaching. You have to believe in your system and not waver from it. You can't change it one week, then do something else the next month. You cannot waffle on your convictions. You have to stand for something and stick with it and let it grow. In my case I have only been a head coach for two years, but I have not changed much. Change sometimes can be good, but too much change usually is not good—unless things aren't working well. I didn't make many changes from year one to year two. I tried to build on things we did the first year, enhance things.

Even though I've only been a head coach for two seasons, this is my sixth season as an Eagle. I feel I have some roots in Philadelphia and with this organization, so I've tried to educate myself on the history of the team and get to know some of the former Eagles who are still in the area.

It's been good to get some of the former players involved, inviting them to alumni days or to a practice or game. They love it, and I want them to feel a part of the team. They own a part of our championship because they paved the way for us to do what we did. So I am always appreciative of those guys.

I see Dick Vermeil and Ron Jaworski. I became friends with Vince Papale and Harold Carmichael when I was a player here. When we left Philly for Cleveland, Vince's wife, Janet, pitched in and helped sell our house. We always stayed in touch after that, and she helped us buy our next house when I came back. Our kids are about the same age as their kids are, so we had a connection there. We are members of the same country club, and we have done a lot of things together. It has been a good bond. They are dear friends.

I feel like I'm supposed to be here. I've talked about God's plan for my life, about this journey, and the people I've met along the way. I have been given some opportunities, and it's up to me to make the most of them. With God's help, I'll continue to do so.

CHAPTER 13

JOURNEY TO THE SUPER BOWL

You don't become a Super Bowl champion with one play. It takes hundreds of plays and thousands of hours of study, practice, and hard work. It takes sixteen regular season games, and then the playoffs. So my emphasis in 2017 was trying to keep our team focused on the tasks in front of us and not the end result.

It was interesting the way our schedule was broken up. We had three home games in a row starting in late October against the Redskins, 49ers, and Broncos. So I just broke it down and said, "We've got this three-game stretch coming up at home. We're going to take them one at a time, and keep all of our energy on these three home games. And then we are going to have a bye."

I kept giving them blocks. When we went on a three-game road trip in early December, I said, "We've got three games here, guys. I don't care about anything but these next three weeks. Let's commit to these next three weeks to get the job done. And then we will worry about the next stretch after that."

Doing it that way—making them focus on a slice of the pie at a time—isn't as overwhelming as looking at all sixteen games at once. I think that approach really did help us get through some of the tough times that we had during the season.

September 10—Eagles 30, Redskins 17

Before our season opener, we kept hearing from the media that we had lost five straight games to the Redskins. They were saying the Redskins had our number. So that motivated us a little. It gave me some great team meeting speeches. As I mentioned, there were also the comments made by Michael Lombardi, questioning my ability as a coach. I was mad and a little disappointed, but I tried to hide it. I was thinking, "Now what happens if we lose the game? What are people going to say then? They might say Michael Lombardi was right."

When we got to FedEx Field, our guys were jacked and ready to go. On third down and twelve during our first series of the game, Carson Wentz spun out of two tackles and hit a wide-open Nelson Agholor for a touchdown. It was just an incredible play to start the year.

Our defense kept us in the game. We had a strip sack and recovery by Fletcher Cox with less than two minutes left. He ran it back for a touchdown and we won the game. It was a great way to get the monkey off our back.

But we also had a couple of injuries in the game. We lost our starting corner, Ronald Darby, who we had just traded for during camp, with a dislocated ankle. And then we lost our kicker Caleb Sturgis. As the head coach I had to face the reality of these losses. Darby ended up missing nine weeks, and Sturgis missed the rest of the season. But I still felt that we were going to have a chance. We were going to be better than 7–9. I am a big believer in not putting yourself in a box and saying, "We're going to be 8–8, 10–6, 11–5." But I knew we were better than we were the year before. Despite the injuries, I felt really good about the opportunity that was in front of us.

September 17—Chiefs 27, Eagles 20

This game was the one I was anticipating the most, going back to Kansas City and facing Andy Reid. I was really nervous. I knew when I looked across the field what would be going through his mind. When he coaches, he wants to put a dagger in the opponent's heart. That's what Andy preaches all the time. He would have exhausted all the film on Jim Schwartz and our defense, and he would know our defense inside and out.

The media was playing up the angle about the student going back to face his teacher. But I wasn't playing Andy Reid. I had to remind myself of that. I was playing the Kansas City Chiefs. I was game planning against Bob Sutton and that defense. I worked with Bob Sutton for three years, so I kind of knew how he thought. The game was just a matter of executing and putting our guys in position to be successful.

Andy and I met up on the field and small-talked, and congratulated each other on the start of the season. He asked how Jeannie was doing. I asked how Tammy was. Then it was time.

It was a really good game, with back-and-forth early on. We missed a field goal, and it hurt us. But the score was tied at thirteen well into the fourth quarter. Then they scored two touchdowns in a little more than four minutes to put the game out of reach.

Andy and I shook hands after the game, and he was very complimentary. I really appreciated it. He reminded me that we still had a good football team and told me what he had told me many times: "Keep being you."

We were having success throwing the ball in the game, and that's what I wanted to keep doing. But I knew in order to win the game I was going to have to call more run plays. I hadn't against the Chiefs, and I put the team in a bad situation. Carson was intercepted twice in the fourth quarter. I learned a valuable lesson in that game. You can't win the game with one play. I shouldn't have put our guys in the position I did. Was it that I wanted to beat Andy Reid? It was probably some of that. I think a little pride got in the way.

In the locker room, I told the team this loss was on me. They played with great effort. I should have done some things differently with play calls and some of the design. I was being ultra-aggressive in the game, and it cost us. This was my loss more than the team's loss.

After that, I made some decisions about play calling that probably changed the course of our season.

September 24—Eagles 27, Giants 24

This was an emotional game. We lost Darren Sproles for the season with a broken forearm and knee injury. We jumped out to a fourteen-point lead, and then the Giants scored twenty-one unanswered points. It was like, "Whoa, what just happened?" Our third quarter was one of the worst quarters we had all season long. It was the first time some of the players were getting chippy with one another on the sideline.

I knew the offense needed to make some plays in the fourth quarter to help us win the game. The score was tied at twenty-four when we took over with thirteen seconds left. Carson hit Alshon Jeffery on the sideline for nineteen yards, and there was one second left. I had to decide if we should punt from the Giants' forty-three or attempt a sixty-one-yard field goal with Jake Elliott, our rookie kicker who had missed a field goal in the Kansas City game. His best kicks in pregame were from about fifty-four yards, and that was with no rush. He has a lot of confidence. That's what I love about him. I asked him if he could make it, and he said he could. "Let's kick it," I said

Odell Beckham was back in the end zone in case the kick was short. He was hoping to run it out. But when Jake hit that ball, man, boom! That thing sailed, hung up in the air, and went through the uprights. Everybody charged the field. It was a great moment. It felt like we just won the Super Bowl.

I think it changed the course of our season. And it changed the course of the Giants' season, because things went the other way for them after that. That game was the start of a nine-game winning streak for us. The year before, we probably would have lost that game. When things like that start happening, you get the sense that maybe this is your year. Those thoughts started creeping into our minds. But we started the previous season 3–0, so I didn't take anything for granted.

Jake was a great addition to our team. After we lost Caleb in the first week, we brought in some kickers for a tryout but didn't feel good about any of them. Jake had been drafted by the Bengals and had been on their practice squad, so we never had the opportunity to work him out. So once we acquired him, all we could evaluate him on were his preseason kicks. I'm glad we were able to sign him. He has a bright future and is a great kid.

October 1—Eagles 26, Chargers 24

This was our first West Coast trip, so I talked to our sports science and strength and conditioning guys to plan the best approach to travel. Based on information I found, it was most beneficial for us to leave on Saturday, the day before the game. We left about two hours earlier than we normally would. I let the players travel in sweat suits so they would be more comfortable on the plane. And once we got to the hotel at about 3:30 LA time, I had our strength and conditioning guys lead them through about fifteen minutes of core and stretching exercises to get the blood flowing. I tried to keep our schedule close to East Coast time. We had curfew at 9:30 p.m. West Coast time, which is 12:30 East Coast time.

We woke up the next day and everyone was fresh and ready to go. We got to the stadium, and I noticed most of the players were bouncing off the walls. There was a lot of energy. In the game, we featured our running game, and LeGarrette Blount really took off as the game went on.

He's a bigger back, and he's physical. As we wore them down up front, their guys on the back end didn't want to hit him anymore. He had some really nice runs to finish off the game, giving him his best performance of the season with 136 yards and an average per carry of 8.5 yards. He was a great asset, a great pickup for us.

October 8—Eagles 34, Cardinals 7

We scored on our first three possessions of the game, and we were leading 21–0 in the first quarter. The confident swagger was starting to come out. We were starting to catch our stride at this point and becoming the team I thought we could be.

Carson made some tremendous throws in that game. Torrey Smith had a big touchdown. Nelson Agholor took the Nestea Plunge into the end zone for the touchdown. Everything really clicked for us in this game.

October 12—Eagles 28, Panthers 23

This was a Thursday night game, and everyone was saying this was our first real test of the season. We were going against a really good defense, and Cam Newton was trying to get his stride after surgery in the spring. We were going against a well-oiled machine. Ron Rivera was going to have those guys ready to play.

Pete Morelli was the referee in that game. We scored a touchdown and kicked the extra point in the third quarter, but the Panthers were penalized for an illegal formation. Instead of giving me the option of electing to go for two, he just assumed I would take the point and have the penalty yards assessed on the upcoming kickoff. So both teams cleared the field. I said, "Pete, look at me!" I pointed to my eyes. He said, "What?" I said, "I want to go for two." Because of the penalty we had the ball on the one-yard line instead of the two. We got the two-point conversion and went up by eight.

Even though I had previously gone for it on fourth down in games leading up to that one, that was the first time I had made the decision that I wanted to take the point off the board to go for two. I wanted to send a message to our players and obviously the opponent that we were in it for the long haul.

Our defense rose to the occasion in that game. Jalen Mills,

Nigel Bradham, and Mychal Kendricks all had big games. The defense created turnovers and we got after their quarterback. That was a milestone game for us, going up against a really good opponent and on a short week on the road.

October 23—Eagles 34, Redskins 24

This was the first game where Carson wowed everybody with his athleticism. He was hit in the pocket and it looked like he was going down, but he popped out and scrambled for seventeen yards. On another play, he was getting dragged down and he threw a nine-yard touchdown pass to Corey Clement in the back of the end zone. Our offense was really catching its rhythm.

But this was a bittersweet day. We lost two starters for the season—our Pro Bowl left tackle, Jason Peters, and our starting middle linebacker, Jordan Hicks. I'll never forget the whole stadium chanting "Jason Peters!" That's the love they have for him. But now we were down three starters plus our kicker and it was beginning to take its toll. Everyone was wondering how much more we could weather and still overcome.

October 29—Eagles 33, 49ers 10

We were coming off an emotional game with the Redskins and playing on a short week after a Monday night game. We were playing against an opponent that had been struggling, and a lot of times you play down to their level. Sometimes you can even have a letdown. I know that having been on many teams where that happened. So I kept telling the players during the week to guard against a letdown. I told them they needed to create energy and bring it every single day.

Sure enough, we started the game poorly. And it was frustrating. I was furious. As I mentioned, I was mic'd up that game, so I had to be careful about some of the words I used. I told the offense to pull their heads out of their butts. I got after the coaches and I got after the players. I felt it was my job to rein everybody in and get the problems fixed. Our guys responded and bounced back in the second half, and we found a way to win. Jalen Mills had a pick-six that punched our ticket.

November 5—Eagles 51, Broncos 23

This was the last game before the bye. If we could win this game, we would be 7–1. If not, we'd still be 6–2 and in control. The Broncos had a tremendous defense. They were ranked number one in the league at the time. They had a swarming secondary. We had an early touchdown to Alshon, and from there everything just clicked. The offensive line prided itself on being physical, and they played a great game.

We had a big lead late, so this was a chance for Nick Foles

to get in the game. He threw a ball to Nelson Agholor late in the fourth quarter that went for thirty-five yards to the four-yard line. We scored on the next play. To put fifty-one points against the number-one defense in the league was pretty special. Our players did a nice job of not only preparing during the week but also executing the plays on Sunday.

November 19—Eagles 37, Cowboys 9

The previous year, we came off the bye and started losing games, so it was a concern again going into the Dallas game. I felt we had a good opportunity to make a nice run, not only for the rest of the regular season but also in the postseason.

I had started using the phrase "faceless opponents" a couple of weeks earlier in a team meeting. At this point, I started using the term a lot. I told the team it didn't matter who was on the other side of the ball, or whether their helmets had horses or stars or cardinals on them. They were faceless opponents. We needed to focus on ourselves and our jobs. That kind of became our mantra for the rest of the season.

We had lost to Dallas in overtime on a Sunday night game the year before. And here we were in Dallas playing in another Sunday night game. I kept reminding them of that. We struggled offensively at the start, but our defense kept us in the game. We were losing 9–7 at halftime. There was no panic, though.

Instead, it was the first time all season I saw the players rallying around each other, saying, "We're going to be okay. Let's just keep doing our jobs. We're going to be fine. Just eliminate the mistakes. Let's just focus on our assignments." The players were doing it. It wasn't anything the coaches were saying. We didn't make any major adjustments at halftime. We just tried to improve what we were doing in the first half. We scored thirty unanswered points in the second half of the game.

November 26—Eagles 31, Bears 3

To me, the Bears were a scary opponent. They were not playing very well and had nothing to play for, except to be a spoiler. So we had to understand they were a faceless opponent. We needed to dominate them. We were able to do that, and we didn't fall into the trap. I think we learned from the 49ers and the Cowboys games that we couldn't let up.

We kept hearing everything was coming too easily for us. The media said nobody was challenging the Eagles. I took the opposite approach. I told our team we were pretty good, and that we earned our record. In the National Football League, every opponent is worthy.

December 3—Seahawks 24, Eagles 10

We felt comfortable and confident going into the game, but it didn't come off that way. We missed a wide-open Nelson Agholor for a potential touchdown. Offensively we did some things out of character. We were a little undisciplined on defense and we gave up a couple of big plays. We fumbled the ball in the end zone as we were about to score. It just wasn't us.

I took the blame on that one, took it on my shoulders. I told the team we needed to learn from it, and that I had to do a better job of preparing them during the week.

December 14—Eagles 43, Rams 35

After the loss in Seattle, we went straight to the airport and flew to LA to prepare for the Rams in the Los Angeles Memorial Coliseum the next week. We spent the whole week in LA instead of flying back to Philly and then flying cross-country back to LA again. We had a really good week of practice. When you are on the road and you are in LA you worry about distractions. But I had a curfew, and everything worked well. Our guys really embraced the week. They enjoyed being in the sun in LA in December. This was when Kobe Bryant, a Philly native, talked to the team, on Friday.

We came away with a hard-fought win against a good

team. But it was also bittersweet because we lost our starting quarterback. As I described earlier, Nick came in and helped us win that game, and we clinched the NFC East title.

December 15—Eagles 34, Giants 29

We were still playing to win the NFC and for home-field advantage throughout the playoffs. That was our motivation in this game. We knew we were a better team, but still, it was the Giants and we were at the Meadowlands, so anything was possible. They came out in a no-huddle offense and went up and down the field. They took a 20–7 lead.

Things got a little tense on our sidelines. When teams spend so much time together, there is going to be some of that, especially late in the year. Some of it can be healthy. This was the healthy kind, and it worked out for us. It was a great team victory on the road. In Nick's first start he threw four touchdown passes, and everybody thought he was the greatest thing.

December 25—Eagles 19, Raiders 10

Our offense wasn't at its best in this one, but the defense kept us in the game. Jake Elliott kicked a field goal to tie it, and then another to give us the lead in the fourth quarter.

And then Derek Barnett picked up a fumble and brought it back for a score.

It wasn't a pretty win. We were a much better football team than the Raiders, but we didn't play like it that day. One of our goals going all the way back to training camp was to win the NFC and get home-field advantage throughout the playoffs. What a great gift it was to do it on Christmas Day.

December 31—Cowboys 6, Eagles 0

I wanted to rest a few of the starters in this game and play some others maybe a quarter or so. A lot of backups played a good portion of the game. It was the first time all season we were shut out, and we didn't capitalize on opportunities. It was disappointing.

We had a chance to have the most wins in franchise history at fourteen. So we were on the verge of Philadelphia Eagles greatness. But we had already wrapped everything up. So 13–3, I'll take it. I'll take it every year.

At the end of the day we said, "You know what, we're NFC East champs. We secured home-field throughout. We've got a first-round bye. Everything is still right in front of us, even though the outside world was saying we wouldn't get out of the divisional round of the playoffs."

January 13—Eagles 15, Falcons 10, Divisional Playoff Game

Going into the divisional round against Atlanta, my confidence was at an all-time high. I knew Nick was settling in as the starter. Believe it or not, until we got to the postseason Nick never had any real reps with the starters in practice. After the first two weeks of training camp, he didn't do any work because of an elbow injury. Then he had no practice reps during the preseason, and he played in only one preseason game.

When Carson was healthy during the regular season, Nick only worked with the service team. My philosophy is to give the starter all the practice reps, so Carson got them all.

After Carson went down and Nick became the starter, we were only having walk-through practices. I thought that was what the team needed at the time. Late in the season, I typically pull the pads off to try to keep the team fresh. If I could do it over again, I don't know if I would have put the pads back on late in the regular season, but I would have made the practices high tempo.

I was taking our situation for granted, thinking a veteran quarterback could process the information without the reps. But Nick wasn't getting to see receivers run full speed, and he wasn't passing against live coverage. During the bye week before our first playoff game, I went back to live practices because I knew Nick needed to experience the live bullets, get his timing and accuracy, and feel the pocket.

I wasn't the only one thinking we needed to put the pads back on. The leaders on my player council asked for it too. They wanted more physical practices. I was glad they brought it up, because it convinced me it was the right thing to do.

By that time, I had about three weeks to study Nick and the things that made him successful during his Pro Bowl season in 2013. As I explained earlier, I also spent some time with him and asked him what he enjoyed doing. I wanted to know what he thought the game plan should look like. Nick and I were developing a play caller–quarterback connection. You begin to feel what the quarterback really likes or what he enjoys executing out on the field. So we tailored the game plan for him. You could see Nick getting better and better in each game of the postseason right up through the Super Bowl.

We weren't going to take the Falcons lightly. They were in the Super Bowl the year before. They had a powerful offense and a great young defense. We struggled a little bit early in the game. We had some costly turnovers. We caught our stride in the second half of that game as far as the passing game went. Nick really took off. We had some bigger plays.

In the first quarter we were dead-on into the wind, making it tough to throw the ball. And at the end of the game we were with the wind. We had a five-point lead late in the game, and the Falcons marched it right down the field. They converted a fourth and six on a nice pass to Julio Jones. They got to the two-yard line and our defense came up extremely big on a play that basically won the game for us.

This is the game where Lane Johnson and Chris Long put on the dog masks. The underdogs won.

January 21—Eagles 38, Vikings 7, NFC Championship Game

We were playing the number-one defense in the league for the second time. The first time was against the Broncos. We had our work cut out for us in this game, and I was nervous. I went into the game thinking I had to stay aggressive against that defense. We had to attack it, and that's what I preached.

On the first drive we had a miscommunication on defense, and they got their tight end on a linebacker. It ended up being a touchdown into the corner. We got that fixed, and then some. We scored thirty-eight unanswered points. We kept them off-balance with the run and pass, and their defense had no idea what was coming. Our offensive line play was outstanding. Our defense buckled down, and Patrick Robinson had the pick-six.

In the third quarter I called a flea-flicker that resulted in a forty-one-yard touchdown from Nick to Torrey Smith. There's a funny story there. When I worked for Andy Reid in Philadelphia, his assistant was Carol Wilson. She's retired now, but she had worked for a lot of coaches in Philadelphia.

On Monday nights back then, the offensive coordinator, wide receivers coach, and I would write the game plan on the grease board. Each week, Carol would sit at the conference table with her laptop and type the game plan for us off the grease board. She couldn't read my writing, so I'd walk her through it. We had a category called specials, and we'd put some gadget plays in there. Each week, Carol would ask me about the flea-flicker. It was her favorite play. She just loved it.

Fast forward to the NFC Championship Game. We needed another gadget play. I had a flea-flicker play on my board for months that I had never put in. Well, when Frank Reich brought me a rough draft of our game plan, it had the flea-flicker in there. At that point, it brought me back to Carol.

A few days before the game, she texted me: "It's Carol. Been a long time. Just wanted to reach out and say congratulations. See, good things happen to good guys. My only suggestion is to use the flea-flicker. Give my best to Jeannie." I texted her back: "Hey, Carol, by the way, the flea-flicker is finally in the game plan this week. I know—just have to call it." She sent me a thumbs-up back.

After the game, I did my media thing and I came back to my office. I had something like 125 text messages. I scrolled down and saw that I had one from Carol. It said, "Now you see why I wanted the flea-flicker in the game. So happy for you." I texted her back, "You finally got your wish, Carol."

The play didn't work like we practiced it during the week, though. In the game Nick handed off to Corey Clement, and he pitched back to Nick. But we had never practiced with Corey. It was always with either Jay Ajayi or LeGarrette Blount. When Corey was on the field, he pitched it high to Nick, and Nick had to reach to get it and sidestep to throw the ball to Torrey. At that point, when we hit that play, I knew we had them.

In practice, Nick threw the deep ball to Alshon, where it was supposed to go. Later, when I asked why he threw it to Torrey, he said, "I saw where Harrison Smith was, and I knew exactly what we were asking Torrey to do. Torrey ran a perfect route. I just trusted him and threw it to a spot." Torrey did an excellent job working toward the catch and hitting the pylon and bringing it in for the touchdown.

The thing that stands out about that game is that all of our free agents that we signed in the spring contributed. It was Nick and Torrey. It was Chris Long disrupting the pass so that Patrick Robinson could intercept it and go the distance. Alshon Jeffery and LeGarrette Blount had touchdowns.

Very few people gave us a chance in that game. But we didn't listen to the noise. We just focused on our jobs and found a way to win another game.

CHAPTER 14

THE OTHER SIDE OF SUCCESS

Three days after the Super Bowl, we had our final team meeting of the season. The first thing I did was to congratulate the entire organization—players, coaches, and administrators. I reflected a little on what we had accomplished, talking about the resiliency of the team, how we dealt with adversity and overcame so much.

Then I focused on the future—the immediate future as well as the long-term future. I told them this would be the last time this group of men would ever be together, and that our team would not be the same tomorrow. Change would be inevitable.

I talked about the other side of success. What does it look like? I wondered aloud if we would be able to remain focused on our team, or if the focus would shift to individual priorities. I asked them if they thought their off-the-field opportunities might cut into their preparations for the 2018 season. I questioned if they were going to be able to say no to family and friends when their requests were getting in the way of what was best for the Eagles. I asked if their contracts would become more important than their commitments.

I wanted them to understand that it would take everybody to make another run. The target had just gotten extremely large on our backs. Everybody would be shooting for the world champions. I did not plan on being the one-and-done team. No, they needed to plan on playing football from August until February. It's the new norm in Philadelphia.

The last thing I told them is they needed to appreciate what they accomplished. They needed to enjoy it. We celebrated the Super Bowl. It's important that you remember where you came from, what got you here, and not just the high points, but the low points, the struggles, too. But once that championship banner was hung on the wall, the 2017 season was over. Put it to bed.

When we gathered again in April, my goal was to refocus the group and make sure they understood our record wasn't 16–3 anymore. It was 0–0. They couldn't do this Super Bowl glide into the new season. After all, a lot of our success in 2017 came about because of what we did the previous offseason.

The threat of complacency is what concerned me most. Complacency probably is the number-one evil in our sport, especially for teams that have won a championship. As a leader, I need to reinforce that there is no substitute for hard work and preparation. I can't take shortcuts in my job. I can't shorten a day, or take away plays in an off-season practice, or go without pads in training camp. It's too easy to say I've been there and done that so I don't have to put in the work. Sometimes it takes getting beat or getting your lip bloodied for guys to understand that. I'm hoping we can avoid that.

I won't let up on them at all. In fact, I'll go harder. A great way to send a message to your team is with the physicality of practice. I will be firmer going forward until everybody buys back into what we're doing, and understands the whys.

I liked the way Mike Holmgren handled things in 1998 after we won a Super Bowl in Green Bay, and I am patterning a lot of what I'm doing after what he did. He stayed true to what he believed in. He brought in another group of free agents. We made it back to a second straight Super Bowl and we were favored by eleven points to beat the Broncos. At that point, I think we felt we had arrived and got a little complacent in that game. We began reading our press clippings too much. So we went out and got our tails beat,

31–24. We probably should have won another one. But we did a lot of things well until that last game.

It can be a problem when everyone is telling you how good you are. For the Eagles in 2017, part of the reason we had an edge is everyone doubted us. It was part of our identity. That's gone now. It kind of makes me mad because the same people who doubted us now are telling us how great we are. Coaches can only do so much, but we have to bring awareness and perspective to it all. But the players are the ones who are out in the town and talking to people, listening to what the media is saying. So it can creep into their thinking.

Here is what happens to some Super Bowl winners—they get softened up by all the praise, and then they go against opponents who want to beat them more than ever. Teams play harder against champions. They did it after we won in Green Bay. The Eagles will get everybody's best, as teams will believe they can prove themselves by beating us. We'll get their best play designs, and unscouted looks—maybe a new, creative defense, or a gadget play on offense or special teams. We'll have to be aware of all that. And our focus will have to remain on the Philadelphia Eagles, not our opponents. If we start focusing on our opponents, we will be in trouble.

One of the things that could help us is we have a few veteran players coming back who missed the Super Bowl because of injury—Carson Wentz, Jason Peters, Jordan

Hicks, Darren Sproles, and Chris Maragos. I'm hoping their hunger makes everyone hungry. I can lean on those guys. They can help me rally the troops.

Getting Carson back should give the entire team a big boost. There will be an acclimation period as he takes a little time to get comfortable and confident. But he's the type of player who, with his work ethic, will continue to improve, and before you know it, he will pick up right where he left off.

After the Super Bowl, Howie Roseman spoke with Bill Polian and Jimmy Johnson about how to deal with the Super Bowl hangover. Both of them recommended making some tough decisions and changing the chemistry of the roster. They said if you just remain the same, or make small changes, complacency sets in. Getting five or six new players in free agency can help maintain a competitive edge.

That was part of our thinking. We wanted to create competition, so we went out and signed some veterans. A number of them have played for winners. Michael Bennett and Haloti Ngata have won Super Bowls. Mike Wallace played in a Super Bowl. It's helpful to have guys who have been in the postseason. We're still new at it. To have guys on your roster who have been on other championship teams makes an impact. The rest of the team can feed off that.

Trading for Michael Bennett got a lot of attention. Anytime you can get a player of his caliber, you do it. There is a reason he's a three-time Pro Bowler. When you acquire a guy like him, it makes you better instantly. People have wondered how his personality will fit into our locker room. This is where I trust the culture that we have created. I already have some strong personalities on the team who know to put team first. We do things differently in Philadelphia. Players like Fletcher Cox and Chris Long will embrace a guy like this and show him who we are. Michael has been part of championship teams, so he understands the dynamic. I'm a different coach from Pete Carroll, so he will have to get used to me and my ways. But he's a smart guy.

I feel great about Chris Long coming back. He can still give us valuable playing time, and he had an impact on our team in 2017 on the field and off. He donated his whole paycheck to charities and things he's involved with. He's a great leader that way, and is a positive presence in the locker room.

Haloti is kind of in the twilight of his career, but he still has a couple of good years left. He is a big, physical player who will give us depth. Even though he has accomplished a lot, he understands his role here. We play eight defensive linemen through the game, so they are constantly rotating. He might get fifteen to twenty snaps, and he stays fresh. You need guys like him.

Mike Wallace is replacing Torrey Smith. Torrey is outspoken, but Mike may be even more outspoken than Torrey.

Mike loves to talk trash on the field. That's who he is. He flat-out told me before we signed him, "Coach, I like to talk some trash." But that's okay. It gives him an edge and might fire up the rest of the team. He's a good teammate. He gives us some of the explosiveness we lost with trading Torrey. He's a little better receiver and route runner. He's an excellent slant runner. Speed-wise, they are pretty close.

Mike mentioned to me there were teams that were offering more money than we were but that he wants to be on a championship team. He wants to play with a young quarterback like Carson. That's why you are seeing some of these older players wanting to come to our team. That's a positive of winning—players willing to take less to play here. I'm proud of that as a football coach.

Torrey was a valuable part of our success. He was a big part of the postseason. He had some big catches. He was great in that receiver room. He was very positive in the way he spoke both as a teammate and socially. We decided to trade him mostly because of salary. It was a business decision, but it was a tough one nonetheless.

In addition to acquiring Mike, we are counting on improvement from players who already are on our roster. I expect more from Alshon Jeffery as he continues to work with Carson and gets more on the same page with him. I felt they were just beginning to really understand each other later in the season before Carson got hurt. I want Carson and Alshon to be like Carson and Zach Ertz are in terms of timing.

We allowed 505 passing yards in the Super Bowl, but we didn't think our pass defense was an area that needed an overhaul. A lot of those yards were the result of miscommunications and guys flat-out busting assignments—three for big plays. The guys were playing in the biggest games of their careers, and maybe they lost focus for a second. It's loud, and you're nervous. Maybe you don't hear the call right. Credit Tom Brady for attacking it. But those issues are correctable.

Another player we had to let go was Vinny Curry. He was a player we drafted when I was an assistant for Coach Reid with the Eagles. I've been in his shoes, and I'm excited to watch him play in Tampa Bay.

As I've mentioned, it's never easy letting go of players who have been around a long time, like Brent Celek. He's such a great guy and he did so much for the team and the community. You get attached to certain players, but at the end of the day you have to do what you think is right for the team.

It's hard to replace his leadership. Brent was a guy who came to work every single day and never complained. The next guy will have to step up. It might be Zach Ertz taking on a bigger role and being more of a mentor to the players in the tight ends room and the overall offense.

We lost another tight end in Trey Burton. We knew he

would fetch top dollar as a free agent and there was going to be no way we could match. I spent two years watching him develop. I hated to see him go, but I'm excited for him as he starts his career with the Bears. As a former player, I understand players have to try to get all they can, and this is his opportunity to set up his family for a long time.

Another player who will be missed is LeGarrette Blount. He was a leader who helped us win the championship. We knew we probably weren't going to be able to bring him back, and he signed with Detroit. We felt comfortable with some of our younger running backs. We traded for Jay Ajayi in 2017 and expect he will take on a larger role for us in the 2018 season. Jay can handle the load and is going in as the number-one running back.

The offseason decision that has gotten the most attention from media and fans is bringing back Nick Foles. It is certainly a unique situation because not many Super Bowl MVPs return to their team as a backup. But he is a team player and he is continuing to embrace his role. We knew there was probably going to be some interest in him, so when he and I spoke at the end of the year, I told him that we wanted him back. He expressed how much he loved being here as well. I also made it clear to him that if we were considering a serious offer, we would make sure he was comfortable with it as well.

I'm hoping Nick is with us all season. You want to keep all your good players around. But at the same time, we have seen in the past that circumstances can change. We traded Sam Bradford right before the 2016 season started, so nothing is ever out of the realm of possibility. Ultimately, we are always going to do what we believe is best for the Eagles and for Nick.

Re-signing Nigel Bradham also was big for us. He was a free agent who we felt strongly about. And Nigel didn't want to go anywhere else. He wanted to work something out and stay in Philly. When Jordan Hicks went down during the season, Nigel had to put a lot of hats on as a linebacker. He became the primary signal caller, the guy who lines up the defense, and played two positions on defense without complaining one time. We played a lot of dime defense with Nigel as the only linebacker on the field. He's a tough, smart kid. He's not big, but he's very physical. Now with Jordan back, Nigel will go back to the Sam linebacker position.

Overall, our new team is going to be a lot like our team was in 2017. There is no need to change our methods. I believe the more you do something, the better you get at it. In the book *Outliers*, Malcolm Gladwell says that in order to develop a true expertise, you need to do something for ten thousand hours. There is merit in that. We will find creative ways to make things better, but we aren't going to reinvent anything. We will enhance it. If you are going to change something, there has to be a why.

I had success taking risks with play calling in 2017. I have asked myself if I will be the same type of play caller moving forward, if I will have the same aggressive nature. I want to say yes, I will. It's what I have done and it's what I know. I love putting our team in those situations to be successful. I believe it gives us more of a competitive advantage. But, as I've said, it has to be the right situation in order for me to do that. As the season went on, I gained knowledge from week to week, and I was able to compile the lessons that make me improve. Hopefully that will help me in my third year.

I'm not real concerned about the league catching up to what we do offensively, which is a little different from most teams. We use many different personnel groups and formations. We do a great job of self-scouting. With the way we structure our game plan, if an opponent takes away one thing, it will open up another. As long as we maintain a good balance with run and pass, teams might have an idea of what we like to do, but they won't know what's coming or when it's coming.

We will look to enhance our package of run/pass options. We studied it hard this spring to try to make it more unique and to be able to use it with different personnel groups and from different formations. Our challenge as coaches is to make sure our RPO game matches up with our screen game, our play-action pass game, and our quarterback movement game outside of the pocket. The challenge is to make it all look the same.

Our offensive coaching staff has changed, so there has been a feeling-out process going on. Frank Reich was valuable to me. He's a smart guy, and he played in the league and coached for a long time. He and I worked together extremely well. He was a big part of the offensive game planning. There were times when I couldn't be as involved with it as much as I wanted to, and he just handled it. We had great communication. It's hard to replace coaches like that.

I think Frank will be a really good head coach with the Colts. He has the personality and the demeanor. He reminds me of myself in the sense that he's going to understand his roster and his players. He'll listen to his players. He's going to be great for Andrew Luck and that quarterback room. He's smart, and his great leadership qualities will have guys gravitating to him. I'm happy for him and know he's going to be successful.

Mike Groh replaced Frank, and he has a great offensive mind. I feel real comfortable with him. He had been our wide receivers coach, and he worked very closely with Frank. He has a great relationship with our offensive line coach, Jeff Stoutland, because they worked together at Alabama.

So he can bridge that gap with the run game. And then he has a great knowledge of the passing game, being a former quarterback at Virginia. This promotion puts him in a bigger spotlight, which is great. If we continue to have success, maybe he'll have an opportunity down the road to become a head coach too.

John DeFilippo, our quarterbacks coach, left to become offensive coordinator for the Vikings. Losing him is tough because he started with Carson as a rookie and has been around our quarterbacks for two years. He's going to a great team, though, so I'm excited for him.

Press Taylor is stepping into John's role. He was the assistant to the quarterbacks coach previously, and then he was an assistant to Mike, working with the wide receivers. So he's going to be really good working with Carson.

Sometimes when coaches win a Super Bowl, they angle for more power. That's the last thing I want. Our infrastructure is really good. If I had more power in the organization, it would take me away from coaching. I'm here to coach. Teaching these guys is my passion. It's hard enough just to coach the team. I want to spend 90 percent of my time on coaching. The other 10 percent, I can help out on personnel. It's not an ego thing with me and never will be. I'm here to serve and help win another championship.

What we have accomplished has been rewarding, but

it's not like my life is complete. I heard an interview with Mack Brown that hit home. He won a national championship at Texas, and he put it in perspective. He said winning a championship is a great achievement, but it's not your life's journey. Your life's journey is about continuing to improve. There is something bigger out there. You haven't accomplished everything there is to accomplish after winning a championship.

This is my twenty-third year in the National Football League as a player and a coach. I don't see myself doing this forever. I'm not sure if my thinking will change as time passes. But the way I see it now, I think I would be content doing this another eight to ten years if I'm blessed enough to last that long. I'd love to do it all in Philadelphia, to be able to stay with one team and do it right, win multiple championships. Then I could retire and have time to spend with Jeannie, my kids, and maybe my grandkids. I could enjoy the twilight years and ride off into the sunset. That's the dream.

ACKNOWLEDGMENTS

Writing this book has been a new kind of journey for me, and as with most journeys, it would not be possible without the love, support, and encouragement of many.

To my beautiful wife Jeannie, I am forever grateful for your love, devotion, countless prayers, and for believing in me as a husband, father, and coach. You amaze me by continuing to help me, encourage me, and love me through the ups and downs of life and marriage. You taught me that strength comes from our Heavenly Father, and "with God, nothing shall be impossible." You are my rock and I love you.

To our sons Drew, Josh, and Joel, thank you for being by my side through this journey. I'm so proud of you. You inspire me to be a better man. I love you so much.

To my mom and my dad, who is now with our Heavenly Father, you are the ones who put me on this course by raising me as a Christian and teaching me family values. I will always be grateful.

Thanks to the many teachers, coaches, teammates, pastors, family members, and friends who have taught me so much about what it means to be a leader, and to believe and to trust in myself. Your fingerprints are on the Lombardi Trophy, too.

I realize it takes the faith and trust of many to win a Super Bowl, including those of you who came before me, and those of you who stood behind me. The people at University of Louisiana-Monroe, you motivated me to chase my dreams. The people at Calvary Baptist-Academy, you inspired me to pursue my passion of coaching and leading young men. Jeffrey Lurie, you trusted me and then led our organization with an emotional intelligence that helped bring a championship to the great city of Philadelphia. My sincere thanks to all of you.

To my agent Bob Lamonte, thank you for providing me the opportunity to become a head coach in the NFL. To Dan Pompei, I am grateful for your tireless work in bringing my story to these pages. And to Mauro DiPreta and Hachette Books, I'm appreciative of you believing in this journey.

My hope is this book will inspire others to follow their hearts and dreams and to never give up, no matter the circumstances.

"Fearless"

Fear not, for I am with you;

Be not dismayed, for I am your God.

I will strengthen you, Yes, I will help you,

I will uphold you with My righteous right hand.

Isaiah 41:10

PHOTO CREDITS